World Tree Story

History and legends of
the world's ancient trees

World Tree Story

History and legends of
the world's ancient trees

Julian Hight

www.worldtreestory.co.uk

For Charlotte, Jake and Harry

Another day of screaming trees,
The echoing crack, resounding thud,
Successive giants crash on mud;
The piteous silence, now no breeze,
Can sing or russle through these trees.

From *Forest Farewell* by Pauline Hight (1934-2010)

World Tree Story – history and legends of the world's ancient trees

ISBN: 978-0-9932906-0-2

First published in the United Kingdom in 2015 by Julian Hight

Volume copyright © Julian Hight 2015
Text copyright © Julian Hight 2015
Images copyright © Julian Hight 2015 (except where stated)
The moral rights of the author have been asserted.

A CIP catalogue record for this book is available from the British Library.

Design and artwork by Julian Hight: www.julianhight.co.uk
Edited by Anna Carr: www.littleblackdot.co.uk

ABOVE: The Seasons, Louise Hight 2010 www.louisehight.co.uk
FRONT ENDPAPER: Foxtail Pines, Inyo National Forest, California, USA 2014
BACK ENDPAPER: Wyndham's Oak, Silton, Dorset, England 2012

Printed in China by Imago on paper sourced from sustainable forests.

For further information, or to order this book direct from the publisher visit the website:
www.worldtreestory.co.uk

Contents

Introduction

The first trees, Archaeopteris, are thought to have appeared on the planet around 370 million years ago. They proceeded to clothe the Earth in dense forest, absorbing high levels of carbon dioxide and producing oxygen, thereby laying down the roots enabling a breathable atmosphere for mammals to exist.

Today Archaeopteris is extinct, but its present day descendants have developed into myriad shapes and sizes with unique and differing characteristics, in response to their particular localised and varied environments.

The destinies of trees and people are inextricably linked. Trees provide timber, fuel, fruit, medicine and shade in everyday life. They develop, enrich and anchor soil, trap carbon dioxide and refresh the air with oxygen. They offer natural, powerful water-retaining properties for flood prevention. They also inspire awe and wonder. Throughout the world, native peoples have worshipped, written stories and poems, and lived worked and died amongst ancient trees. They are living links to the ancestors and history of the local community, green monuments spanning multiple generations of human life.

With us they share many characteristics: growing from seed, through youth to maturity, and into decay before finally and inevitably succumbing to death and collapse. Like us, they are both individuals and part of their community, exhibiting unique character, which they carry with them for their lifetime – often a thousand years or more – before rotting back into the earth from whence they came (if allowed), in turn becoming host to a myriad of life-forms in the process.

The balance between native communities and their environment has skewed. Trees and forests suffer at the hands of an ever expanding human population, keen to keep pace with a spiralling and seemingly unending appetite for development, driven by short term economic gain rather than long term environmental concerns.

The inspiration for this book

On 1st July 1863, my great great grandfather Henry Hight – a farmer from Northamptonshire – set sail for Timaru, New Zealand, in search of new horizons and the promise of a good life.

With his wife Elizabeth and their three children, they boarded the Lancashire Witch at Gravesend near London. The journey lasted three months, paid in part by the British Government with the balance by promissory note. It was not long before scarlet fever broke out and claimed the lives of three adults and twenty three children. All were buried at sea. Due to the disease the Lancashire Witch was refused permission to land for provisions at the Cape of Good Hope, and when she finally arrived at Lyttleton the ship was quarantined. The passengers were dismayed to find little or no provisions or arrangements for their reception. Nine babies had been born during the voyage.

This must have been a hugely disappointing start to their vision of a brave new world, but it was a harbinger of the harsh realities that were to follow. Mid-nineteenth century New Zealand could be a fairly inhospitable place, in parts lawless, and still in the throes of the infamous northern Maori wars. Only hard work and a dogged determination saw the Hight family forge a living farming cattle near Christchurch, to support their dream of a new life.

Some one-and-a-half centuries after Henry and

his family took their pioneering steps, I resolved to follow their footfalls and embark on a voyage to the other side of the world.

Brave new world

It is a mark of the changes that have taken place in the intervening years, that my journey took only three days as opposed to three months, and to my knowledge, nobody died. I travelled via Hong Kong and returned via Singapore, visiting south-eastern Australia and Tasmania as part of the bargain. I was almost immediately struck by the fact that I was following a long-trodden colonial trail.

The pioneers may be long gone, but their legacy survives in the westernisation of the places where they traded, and continue to trade in a modern guise. Western designer brands sit not uncomfortably alongside eastern traditional shops, as modern technology shares the streets and waterways with rickshaws and Chinese junks.

It is precisely the ability to change that has developed each race's distinct culture and unique character, and the same can be said for the trees of the world. Many species are native only to their distinct locality, especially where they grow on isolated lands cut-off from the rest of the world. They have adapted to suit their specific climate and environment. That is why it is important that countries worldwide retain national monopolies of native plant and tree species. Individual ecosystems evolve over hundreds and thousands of years developing a natural balance between the animal and plant kingdoms. Each species becomes reliant and interdependent on the other. For example koalas in Australia feed exclusively on only one species of Eucalypt leaf. The great New Zealand Kauri trees thrive under cover of native Manuka to

ABOVE: Dinton Beeches, Wiltshire, England 2011

develop as young trees. Banyan trees – the strangler figs – can only reproduce with the help of native fig wasps. These are natural, symbiotic relationships.

It is only relatively recently in our history that tree diseases and pests have crossed international borders with ease, catching a lift on foreign imports. Cases in point are Ash Dieback, thought to have originated in Poland, now entrenched throughout Europe, and the Emerald Ash Borer, originally from Asia, now boring its way through North America's Ash population, to name but two.

Sources and travel

I endeavoured to travel widely over five years to document and photograph the subjects included in this volume. I am indebted to certain friends and colleagues on whom I bestowed assignments when I heard that they were travelling to a destination I had not yet managed to visit. A good starting point for each subject was to search for an old photograph or engraving. I had had first-hand experience of this whilst researching my first book Britain's Tree Story. Victorian photographers captured famous landmarks for the then-thriving British postcard industry, leaving a legacy of

7

images of a century passed. I was astonished at how widely-travelled the artists and photographers of the nineteenth and twentieth centuries were when I came to procure world subjects. There was no shortage of material, all corners of the globe seemingly well covered – surprising when you consider the perils of travel a century ago compared to the relative ease of travel today. This is perhaps a reflection of the human nomadic spirit, the desire to travel to pastures new (whether by necessity or choice), a spirit which has been with us since the first people resolved to leave Africa, in time populating the entire planet with the exception of only the most inhospitable climes. Trees spread their seed in other ways – via wind, water, through animals and birds, but the outcome is the same: life excels – where it can.

Colonialism and empire

British and European pioneers set off primarily seeking new land, resources and riches – having long used up most of their home reserves. Trees were prime booty and considered worthy of shipping halfway around the globe for the profits they delivered from their timber. All too often excessive felling occurred, trees being viewed simply as commodities for the taking, a practice that sadly continues to this day along the equatorial

rainforest belt and beyond – the last great forest reserves.

Felling of primary British forests is such a distant memory that the current rural landscape of rolling hills and open fields is largely considered natural. The truth is that most of it was cleared for agriculture over a period of many centuries, and while it may never have been continuous dense woodland, (interspersed as it was with wood pasture, rough grass and heath land), the fact that Britain currently has only 2% ancient native woodland cover speaks volumes.

Gods, giants and dwarves

This book tells the tales of 100 of the great survivors of the tree world across 39 countries. From 3,500 year old Giant Sequoia trees and twisted, dwarf-like Bristlecone Pines older still in California; to the venerable, hollow millennial Oaks and prehistoric Yew trees of northern Europe; from ancient Olive trees in the Mediterranean; to the upside down, sacred Baobabs of Africa and Australia and towering Kauris of New Zealand to the god-inhabiting Cedar, Camphor and Cherry Blossoms of mountainous, magical Japan.

Throughout history these great trees have often owed their very survival to the fact that they have provided a livelihood for the people that have lived amongst them, they provided food, shade, fuel and timber in a partnership that has endured for millennia, allowing some trees to obtain millennial status themselves. Stories attach themselves to the trees to the extent that some achieve god-like status, so greatly are they revered by the communities that have lived amongst them.

LEFT: Kauri Gulley, Auckland, New Zealand c1905

In the past century and a half, the balance has shifted. No longer is firewood universally required as an essential fuel, so the age old practice of coppicing and pollarding of trees has rapidly declined, along with the habitat. Cork stoppers are largely replaced by screw-tops in the wine industry which has heralded a major decline in the Mediterranean Cork Oak forests. The demand for cheap paper and wood products is seeing the destruction of the world's last great bands of rainforest across the equatorial belt – paper that could be provided for by sustainable means, given the will. A backlash is in effect promoting sustainability, but as yet is not keeping pace with the loss of fragile, irreplaceable old growth forest.

Consumer power helps – insisting on sustainable products on the high street can have a profound effect on governments and corporations eager to be seen to be doing the right thing.

Individuals versus communities

Recent research has shown that trees exchange nutrients via mycorrhizal fungi. Mycellium – the unseen, branching, thread-like part of fungi which supports its fruiting bodies (like mushrooms) above ground – forms an interconnected super-highway between neighbouring tree roots, and often covers vast areas. It protects, feeds from and distributes nutrients to other trees in the neck of the woods in a mutually beneficial relationship.

The subjects featured here are often individuals, surviving almost as museum pieces due to their epic proportions, immense age or historic or religious importance. In a natural setting, many would act as 'mother' trees, providing for younger or less fortunate members of the wood (and vice versa), a status denied them in humanised environments.

ABOVE: Giant Forest, King's Canyon NP, California, USA 2014

The framework of this book

Ordered by country, broadly as they appear on the global map, from north to south and east to west, the trees are presented in three parts: The Northern Hemisphere, The Equatorial Belt and The Southern Hemisphere. Each contains distinctly different species that have developed uniquely to suit their climate and environment.

I make no distinction between history, fact, legend, folklore and mythology. They all relate to how people have perceived ancient trees throughout history, are intertwined with the life of each tree and its community, and in my opinion share equal validity. They are all a part of the story.

Conservation and preservation

Across the world many esteemed ancient trees survive, synonymous with the history that has unfurled around them. Empires rise and fall, but most of the trees in this book have endured. With them, the human stories, tales and deeds live on.

Their prospects appear grim, and the challenge is to secure their survival. They are a dying breed. Where they have already been lost, regeneration and conservation projects are vital. A thousand year old tree cannot be replaced overnight; that kind of longevity requires 15 or more human lifespans.

Directory of Trees 🍃
See world map overleaf

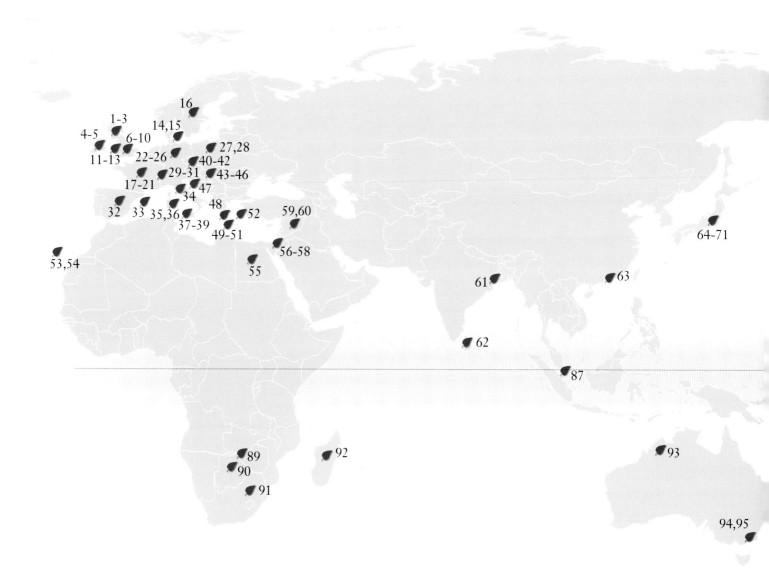

NORTHERN HEMISPHERE

72,73

74-79

80

81

82

83

84

85

86

88

EQUATORIAL BELT

EQUATOR

SOUTHERN HEMISPHERE

96-99

100

The Poker Tree Aberfoyle

Aberfoyle was little more than a quiet Scottish village until Sir Walter Scott put it on the map in 1810 with his novel 'The Lady of the Lake', set around nearby Loch Katrine. Today the town is the gateway to the Trossachs for tourists and visitors heading north.

At a crossroads between the River Forth and the main road to Loch Ard in the shadow of Craigmore hill, stands a twisted veteran Oak *(Quercus petraea)*, with a heavily mossed trunk 2.65m (8.7ft) in girth at its waist, but almost twice that size around its heavily distorted base.

It is known as The Poker Tree, so named after an episode in Scott's novel *Rob Roy*, where the author relates the tale of a fracas at the adjacent inn. Bailie Nicol Jarvie – cousin to Rob Roy – and his two companions enter, despite a stripped willow wand crossing the door – an ancient Scottish symbol warning against entry. A fight ensued against the locals, and Jarvie saved the day by fending off a huge highlander with a hot poker pulled from the fire. The evening ended well however, with much merriment enjoyed by all. In honour of the tale, a poker has traditionally been hung from the tree ever since, and is clearly visible in the 1928 photograph (right).

On my visit however, there was no poker to be seen, and two major branches had recently been lopped, despite a tree preservation order issued by Stirling District Council. That the inn no longer serves its original purpose – having been converted to residential flats – may explain a lack of concern. Successive local landlords and the community of the inn were no doubt responsible for upholding the tradition.

This is Rob Roy country, scene of the deeds and exploits of the celebrated Scottish folk hero who was born just 15 miles (24 km) north of here at Glengyle in 1671, and is a good base to tour the Trossachs and the Queen Elizabeth Forest Park.

As he saw the gigantic Highlander confront him with his weapon drawn, he tugged for a second or two at the hilt of his shabble, as he called it; but finding it loth to quit the sheath, to which it had long been secured by rust and disuse, he seized, as a substitute, on the red-hot coulter of a plough which had been employed in arranging the fire by way of a poker, and brandished it with such effect, that at the first pass he set the Highlander's plaid on fire, and compelled him to keep a respectful distance till he could get it extinguished.

From *Rob Roy* by Sir Walter Scott 1817

ABOVE: The Poker Tree 1928
OPPOSITE: The Poker Tree 2013

The Wallace Yew Elderslie

The great Scottish hero and freedom fighter William Wallace was probably born in Elderslie, just west of Paisley, around 1272. His father, Sir Malcolm, was laird of the estate, where two trees of note with regard to his son flourished. One, known as the Wallace Oak, reputedly sheltered the warrior and 300 of his men in its branches from pursuant English forces. The other is the Wallace Yew, where William is said to have played in its branches as a child. The oak fell in 1856, the victim of a fierce storm, and its remains were gathered and dispersed by relic hunters. The Yew (*Taxus baccata*), or at least a descendent of it, still stands in the brave-heart's childhood garden.

Another legend has the hero planting the yew, but with a girth of 4.3m (14ft), it is generally thought to be no more than 400 years old, meaning it was a sapling long after his death. The estate finally left the Wallace family when it was bought by the Spiers in 1769. They would have welcomed associations with such an historic tree, and may have been responsible for its germination, though there is some speculation on this matter. Yews are known to grow at varying rates according to placement and environmental conditions, and parish records refer to it as "this ancient tree" as early as the 1700s. The tree has also suffered its fair share of torment over the years.

In 1978 a fire set by vandals almost killed it, which motivated Renfrewshire Council to implement a restoration programme. On 12th January 2005 – the 700th anniversary of Wallace's death – a ferocious storm brought half the tree crashing to the ground. Experts feared the worst, but almost a decade on, with the erection of a protective fence and some TLC, Wallace's Yew looks strong once more – a fighter like its namesake, and the centrepiece amongst a monument and ruins of the Wallace household that make a fitting tribute to William Wallace.

In 2011 local dignitaries along with pupils from Wallace Primary School planted a sapling grown from a cutting of the tree in the enclosure beside its parent. Another was planted at the Scottish Parliament building in Hollyrood.

Wallace's gruesome execution – designed to deter future uprisings – in fact had the opposite effect, and culminated in Robert the Bruce's victory against the English at the Battle of Bannockburn in 1314, where he and his soldiers wore sprigs of yew into battle.

It is also worthy of notice, that, in the garden of Wallace's house, there is to be seen a fine specimen of our Scottish yew, said to be coeval with, some say older than, the celebrated oak. But be this as it may, it is certainly of ancient date, and tradition has assigned to it the name of "Wallace's Yew".

From the *Statistical Account for Scotland* 1834-45

ABOVE: 'Wallace the Guardian of Scotland', Wallace Monument, Elderslie 2013
OPPOSITE: The Wallace Yew 2013

The Capon Tree
Jedburgh

Less than 2 miles (3.2km) south of Jedburgh, in a meadow on the south bank of Jed Water, stands the monumental Capon tree, an ancient, sprawling Sessile Oak *(Quercus petraea)*, mossed with age and host to a myriad of life-forms. I noticed that a fox had taken residence and dug his lair inside the hollow trunk – a most distinguished home.

Estimates of its life span range from 500 to 1,000 years, and judging from its waist measurement of 9.37m (30.75ft), I would wager somewhere between the two, taking into account its split trunk which exaggerates its size.

The Oak is said to be lone survivor of the great Jed Forest, which once thrived in the wide, flat, fertile river valley, turned over long ago to agriculture. The weight of the leading, horizontal branch, 3.75m (12.3ft) in circumference – itself the size of a mature oak tree – no doubt caused the tree to split, and is supported by several wooden props.

Where the tree came by its name is uncertain. The general explanation given is that it originates from 'Capuchin', after the monks that lived at Jedburgh Abbey. But there are two other Capon oaks mentioned in antiquity – one at Brampton in Cumbria, the other at Alnwick Castle in Northumberland – and both of these refer to 'Capon' having derived from the Scottish 'Kep' meaning to meet. It is likely that this is the true origin of the name, and reference is indeed made to border clans rallying for action beneath the tree to defend against the English in the sixteenth century. The Jedburgh Callants held a reputation for exceptional bravery, a distinction celebrated each July at the Jedburgh Callant Festival, where a young man is chosen to represent the town and lead a mounted cavalcade to nearby Ferniehurst Castle.

On his return, he passes by the Capon Tree and picks a sprig of the oak to wear in his lapel.

Not far from the Capon Tree atop a hill on the footpath towards the castle, stands a fine, tall and straight English Oak *(Quercus robur)*, known as King O' the Wood. With a girth of 5.6 metres (18.37 feet) it is no match for its distinguished neighbour, but could be old enough to have been a sapling when Mary Queen of Scots stayed at the town in 1566, preceding her eighteen and a half year detention at the pleasure of Elizabeth, whose decisive hands sealed the gruesome fate of the Scottish queen.

This last tree is said to have been the place where the border clans met in olden times ; and hence the name of Capon, from the Scottish word kep, to meet.
From *Arboretum and Fruticetum* by J C Loudon 1838

BELOW: The Capon Tree c1910
OPPOSITE: The Capon Tree 2013

The Palmerston Yew
Palmerston, Dublin

About 4.5 miles (7.3km) west of central Dublin lies the once rural village of Palmerston. A church has stood here, high on the north bank of the River Liffey since pre-Norman times. Ancient burial urns discovered due west in 1868 confirm prehistoric settlement of the area predating the Normans.

In the churchyard, there once grew an ancient Yew, thought to be at least commensurate in age with the earliest church building, making it one of the country's oldest trees. Hollow and ancient, it was blown down in a storm during the 1880s, but not before the Illustrated London News published an engraving from William Wakeman's sketch of the tree in 1864. By that time Stacgory church, built in 1675 on the site of the earlier model, was also in a ruinous state. A short walk off Mill Lane – named after the many mills that utilised the Liffey in the eighteenth and nineteenth centuries – a pathway leads past the old Palmerston tavern, infamous as the scene of the murder of one Laughlin Murphy in 1738. He was killed by Henry Barry, fourth Lord Santry, who received a full pardon for his sins following a reprieve from King George II.

Seven (a significant and magical number in Celtic mythology) younger yews now grow in the churchyard besides several non-native trees scattered amongst the tombstones, most of which are weathered beyond legibility. Palmerston may have been named after Aelred the Palmer who founded a Monastery in 1180 following a pilgrimage to the Holy Land. 'Palmers' returned with palm leaf crosses as mementoes. In Ireland, the practice of scattering them on Palm Sunday was substituted with sprigs of yew, as the tree was revered for its longevity and regenerative properties. Yews were often referred to as palms, so there is every chance the village was named after the old tree.

Ajoining the church, a few yards to the south-eastward, stands a venerable yew-tree, now almost withered, and which has probably given name to the place.
From the *Illustrated London News* 1864

ABOVE: The Palmerston Yew 1864
OPPOSITE: The ruins of Stacgory Church - Yews beyond 2013

Killarney Oakwoods
Killarney National Park, Kerry

It is one deep mass of wood, composed of the richest shades perfectly dipping in the water.
Arthur Young on a trip to Killarney Woods 1776.

In Celtic Ireland, much of the country was covered in vast swathes of forest, which developed steadily following the end of the last ice age around 10,000 years ago. An old saying from the south west of the country 'a squirrel could run from Killarney to Cork without ever setting foot on the ground', is testament to the depth and extent of the woodland.

By the end of the sixteenth century, clearance of the forests had begun in earnest under the reign of Elizabeth I, firstly to deprive Irish rebels of their hiding places, and secondly to reward the English colonists with safe, inhabitable, confiscated lands.

The following century saw further land clearance when farming was deemed more profitable than forest, and oak was used in some degree for ship building – most notably for the East India Company.

But the largest contributor to the destruction of Ireland's forests came from three professions that developed fiercely between the seventeenth and eighteenth centuries, namely those of the cooper, the tanner and the charcoal burner. The Sessile Oaks *(Quercus petraea)*, of southern Ireland were ideally suited to the production of barrel staves, and provided casks for the majority of French and Spanish wines by 1625.

Charcoal burning saw the rapid depletion of Oak woods in Kerry, supplying fuel for local iron works. It took around 600 trees per year to provide charcoal for two smelters in Killarney, which translates to around 8ha (20ac) of Oak forest per annum.

In the eighteenth and nineteenth centuries, bark of Killarney Oaks was stripped in great quantities from live trees to be used for the tanning of animal hides. Unlike the Cork Oak bark harvested in Spain and Portugal which survives the process, Ireland's Sessile Oaks died, so laws were eventually enacted to ensure bark was only taken from felled trees.

The industries declined, and today around 1,400ha (3,500ac) of Oak wood survives in the Killarney Valley around Lough Leane, Muckross and Upper Lakes. They are the most extensive remnants of native woodland in Ireland, protected as a major part of the country's first national park, which was established in 1932.

ABOVE AND OPPOSITE: Oakwood at Muckross

Reenadinna Yew Wood

Killarney National Park, Kerry

Perhaps more remarkable than the Oak wood are the ancient stands of Yew tucked away on the Muckross Peninsula between Muckross Lake and Lough Leane, known as Reenadinna Wood. The dominant species here is that of the Yew *(Taxus baccatta)*, which clings to the limestone reef in shallow soil. Little will grow in the shade of a yew tree, let alone a dense yew wood, with the exception of thick mosses and ivy and the occasional liverwort. So dark is the forest floor, that even yew saplings struggle to get a foothold here.

It was thought that over-grazing by deer was the main root of the problem, despite the yews' poisonous properties, but fencing sections of the wood into deer-free enclosures seems to have had little beneficial effect on its natural regeneration.

Reenadinna Wood is the last remnant of an ancient Yew wood in Ireland, and one of only three remaining in northern Europe. Few individual trees are older than 200 years, but yews are thought to have been growing here continually for around 3-5,000 years.

Yew was felled in the area and used for decorative inlay in furniture manufacturing during the nineteenth century, but 25ha (62ac) of Yew wood survives here in this magical place – twisting, turning, sinuous Yews block out the sunlight and cast ominous shadows and shapes above a luxuriant, spongy, bed of moss. I visited in the pouring rain, which had the effect of turning the trunks and branches shiny and black, lending an almost serpentine appearance.

One day I passed through a wood at West Munster in the west. I took away with me a red yew berry and I planted it in the garden of my court, and it grew up there until it was as big as a man. Then I removed it from the garden and planted it on the lawn of my court even, and it grew up in the centre of that lawn so that I could fit with a hundred warriors under its foliage, and it protected me from wind and rain, and from cold and heat.

Fintan from *The Settling of The Manor of Tara* translated by R I Best 1910

ABOVE AND OPPOSITE: Yew Woods at Muckross

The Muckross Yew

Muckross Abbey, Killarney

People have lived around the shores of Lough Leane since the Bronze Age. The earliest writings are found at Dunloe cave, written in Ogham (the ancient script used by the Druids) which confirms their presence here. During Christian times, monastic buildings appeared. The most important was Innisfallen, built on an island in the lough, and famous for holding the 'Annals of Innisfallen', an eleventh to thirteenth century script telling the early history of Ireland. In 1448, a Franciscan friary was founded by McCarthy Mór, the owner of Muckross, to the east of Reenadinna Wood, within sight of Lough Leanne. In the central cloisters of the abbey stands an ancient Yew *(Taxus baccata)*, with a girth of 3.12m (10.23ft), and a huge arching crown that forms a roof across the open courtyard. Tradition holds that the tree was planted when the abbey was built. Its size may point to a younger tree, but the enclosed space likely directed its energy upwards towards the light rather than outwards, so my guess is that the folklore is right, making the tree over 550 years old, one of the oldest in Ireland. The fact that it has grown only a meter in girth since the 1770s helps confirm this, whilst another Yew standing just outside the abbey walls measuring over 4.5m (14.76ft) in circumference, was probably planted around the same time.

Muckross Abbey suffered a violent history, survived the dissolution of the monasteries, but was finally sacked by Cromwell's forces under Lord Ludlow in 1625. In the 1770s, its only inhabitant was a hermit named John Drake, who accepted pilgrims in return for food. Found reeling drunk one night however, his holy tenancy came to an abrupt end.

In the graveyard are buried local kings from antiquity, joined in the seventeenth and eighteenth centuries by three Gaelic poets: Geoffrey O'Donoghue, Aodhagan O'Rathaille and Eoghan Rua O'Suilleabhain.

A ghostly tale tells of a stranger seen feeding on the corpse of a freshly dug grave by his newly-wed wife. The story is said to have inspired Bram Stoker, who often visited Muckross, to write his classic vampire novel Dracula in 1897.

As a parting thought, if you should decide to visit, be sure not to make off with a memento, as it is said that whoever takes a twig from the Yew will die within a year.

The cloisters form a dismal area, in the centre of which grows the most prodigious yew-tree I ever beheld, in one great stem, two feet diameter, and fourteen feet high, from whence a vast head of branches spreads on every side, so as to perform a perfect canopy to the whole space.

From *A Tour In Ireland 1776-1779* By Arthur Young

ABOVE: The Muckross Yew 1901
OPPOSITE: The Muckross Yew 2013

The Marton Oak

Marton, Cheshire

Not far from the chapel is a very fine Oak, which although but little known, is believed to be the largest in England.

From *Magna Britannia* by Daniel & Samuel Lysons 1810

Britain is renowned for its many great, ancient Oaks which can be found, often in isolation, across the country. The largest girthed and probably oldest living example is a common or Pedunculate Oak *(Quercus robur)*, measuring 14.4m (47.25ft) in girth.

It stands in the garden of a private house in the village of Marton in Cheshire, and according to recent estimates has done so for some 1,200 hundred years. Impossible to date accurately due to an absence of heartwood which has long since rotted away, the fragmented trunk grows as four separate stems, leading some to some believe that it is four different trees. This fragmentation is quite normal for ancient Oaks however, and a common root system confirms that it is but one giant tree. Illustrative and photographic records reveal little change in appearance over three centuries (right).

When The Marton Oak was a sapling, Offa's bloodthirsty reign as Saxon King of Mercia was drawing to an end, and the Viking age was dawning. Local legend has villagers dancing around the tree on May-day, hanging the bark in houses as a good luck charm, and using it to cure skin ailments, including the removal of warts.

In the nineteenth century the hollow trunk was used to tether a bull and keep pigs, when it was still a part of Marton Farm fenced in open fields. But now the tree has a secluded garden feel, and is carefully tended by its custodians. On my visit it had a glorious crown and was brimming with acorns, which until recently were collected by local school children who sold them for 10 pence each in aid of Marton's timber framed church that dates to 1343; a mere 550 years or so younger than the great Oak.

ABOVE FROM TOP: The Marton Oak; c1860, c1900, 1940
OPPOSITE: The Marton Oak 2013

The Darley Dale Yew

Darley Dale, Derbyshire

Derbyshire boasts many ancient trees, including some fine stag-headed Oaks at Chatsworth Park. But the county's oldest and arguably most venerable example can be found in the village of Darley Dale, on the south eastern edge of the Peak District.

The tree in question is a common Yew *(Taxus baccata)*, and stands in the twelfth century churchyard of St Helen's, which it predates by at least a thousand years. The area has held religious significance throughout the life of the tree, two millennia of custom and ritual having centred around it. The lid of a Roman burial urn stands testament to this fact by the chancel doorway. The Romans probably appropriated an already sacred site, as Druidic priests are said to have worshipped amongst groves of Yew – the tree of life – reflecting its regenerative ability and longevity. The Roman poet Lucan appeared shocked by their practices, describing *'every tree sprinkled with human gore'*, where *'birds feared to perch'*. Carving in the shape of the Celtic fertility goddess Sheela-na-Gig can be found in the church. Then, as Christianity took hold, the tree became a symbol of eternal life, the old ways forgotten, consigned to oblivion.

Church Lane, previously named Ghost Lane after the murder of a pedlar in 1635; a leper's window through which the afflicted could witness church services and gravestones adorned with carvings by Huguenots who fled here from France in the mid-eighteenth century all remember the people who have lived and died in Darley Dale. A sun dial was added to the face of the church by the Reverend William Wray in the eighteenth century to encourage the punctuality of churchgoers, who in his opinion spent too much time gossiping beneath the Yew.

The tree itself has changed little. Besides having lost branches which allowed boys to climb onto the church wall and then onto the roof in the early nineteenth century, the girth measured at that time was only slightly less than the 8.31m (27.26ft) that it measures now.

Nor shall thy reverend Yew, the Sire who holds
His sceptre verdant through the changeful year.
Unnoticed stand. He has beheld, like thee.
Thousands entomb'd within his shadow; heard
For ages past the sobs, the heart fetch'd groans
Of parting anguish ere the grave was closed.
And drank the mourner's tears.

From *Reflections* by John Gisborne 1833

ABOVE: The Darley Dale Yew c1920
OPPOSITE: The Darley Dale Yew 2013

The Druid Oak
Burnham Beeches, Buckinghamshire

Burnham Beeches is Slough's 'jewel in the crown', an oasis of calm and antithesis of the largest private industrial estate in Europe. It is a snapshot of old England – a picture of a working forest where the trees were commodities harvested for fire wood by the process of pollarding, a pruning process which effectively lengthened the lives of the trees by promoting re-growth. When coal replaced wood as fuel, Burnham Beeches were saved from the developer's axe by the City of London Corporation who bought the land for 'the recreation and enjoyment' of the people of London in 1890.

Most famed for its collection of ancient, hollow and twisted Beeches, the oldest tree in the forest is in fact The Druid Oak – an ancient, capacious Pedunculate Oak (*Quercus robur*), with a girth 8.9m (29ft), thought to have stood for at least 800 years and quite possibly more.

It almost certainly procured its name in Victorian times, when holidays and days out became commonplace, and romantic visions of a former golden age were embraced.

The fact that the Druids were all but exterminated by the Romans at Anglesey under Suetonius in AD61 some 1,000 years before the tree germinated, should not detract from the suitability of its name. The oral tradition of the Druids may not have left much to posterity, but both Caesar and Pliny recorded contemporary commentaries on the order, the latter describing the '*sacred oaks amongst whose awful shades the Druids strayed.*'

Elsewhere in Britain there are ancient 'Druid Oaks' at Caton in Lancashire and Salcey Forest in Northamptonshire. The very word Druid is thought to have derived from the classical *drys*, meaning Oak, and the Proto-Indo-European *wied*, to see, which together mean *one with knowledge of the oak*, a fitting name for Burnham's most venerable tree.

The druids – that is what they call their magicians – hold nothing more sacred than the mistletoe and the tree on which it grows, provided it is an Oak.
From *Natural History* by Pliny the Elder 1st century AD

ABOVE: The Druid Cult c1914
RIGHT: The Druid Oak 2013
BELOW: The Druid Oak c1910

Nearly in front of the family mansion of John Plumtre, Esq., is a group of oaks known by the names of Majesty, Stately, and Beauty... not perhaps to be equalled by any other of the same nature ; awakening in the mind of the spectator the most agreeable associations of the freedom and grandeur of woodland scenery, with the security and refinements of cultivated life.

From *Sylva Brittanica* by Jacob G Strutt 1824

TOP: Great Oak at Fredville by J G Strutt 1840
ABOVE AND OPPOSITE: Majesty 2014

Majesty Nonington, Kent

The Marton Oak may hold the record for the largest girthed Oak in England, but a tree growing on private land at Fredville Park wins the prize for Britain's largest maiden Oak – that is, a tree that has not been pollarded, and retains its natural towering crown.

Hidden from view in a wooded glade, the giant Oak *(Quercus robur)* fittingly known as Majesty measures 12.2m (40ft) around its waist, and is hollow throughout the length of its 18.8m (61.6ft) tall trunk. As a young boy, local historian Clive Webb remembers climbing into the void and seeing the sky as he looked up.

One of the earliest mentions of the tree appears in 1793, when it was found to measure 9.5m (31ft), meaning it has grown 2.7m (8.8ft) in the interim. Most estimates proffer an age of 5-600 years on Majesty, but its vast size coupled with reports of its mature presence in 1554 – known then as the King Fredville Oak – surely confer a more senior status, especially when compared to some of the other ancient Oaks featured within these pages.

Majesty graces the lawns of Fredville Manor, which passed through the hands of various Norman lords starting with Bishop Odo – infamous brother of William the Conqueror – following the Norman conquest in 1066. It was well placed, equidistant from Dover and Sandwich, two major south-east ports of the day.

By 1746, Margaretta Bridges had had a new house built there. She married John Plumptre four years later, and the family still owns the estate. The house however was destroyed by fire following appropriation by troops during World War II, a catastrophe that Majesty survived. A footprint of the former building is visible in her shadow.

Majesty lost two major branches in 1789, and another in 1926 which left a gaping hole which revealed the tree's cavernous trunk (right). More recently, in 2012, a double V-shaped branch dropped, and leans against the trunk where it fell, like a giant crutch (left).

The legend of the White Horse – a ghostly, equine apparition said to appear on the estate seeking shelter on dark and stormy nights – need only look towards Majesty, and find shelter there beneath the magnificent, voluminous branches of the majestic Oak. She would be hard pushed to find a better retreat.

Harold's Yew

Crowhurst, East Sussex

In the churchyard of St George's, Crowhurst, stands a prodigious ancient Yew *(Taxus baccata)*. Probably the oldest tree in the county of Sussex, sometimes confused with the great Yew at Crowhurst in Surrey, it carries a unique story all its own.

In 771 King Offa gave the lands to the Bishop of Selsey, who built an early church there in gratitude. The manor eventually passed to Harold, England's ultimate Saxon king, in the years leading up to the Battle of Hastings in 1066. William the Conqueror believed that the throne was rightfully his, promised him by Edward the Confessor. But that decision was not Edward's to make, as the laws of the time gave the Witan, a council of Lords and Bishops, that honour. They chose Harold, who Edward is also said to have favoured as heir on his deathbed, but William would not be swayed, and crossed the channel from Normandy to take England.

William totally laid waste to Crowhurst, and reportedly hung the Reeve from Harold's Yew for not disclosing the whereabouts of his treasure, but he spared the town of Battle.

Local historian Nick Austin suggests Crowhurst as the actual site of the Battle of Hastings, not the traditional location at Battle Abbey two miles away. He proposes that the landscape at Battle does not fit descriptions mentioned in contemporary sources, whereas Crowhurst does. The most famous source, the Bayeux Tapestry, illustrates a tree standing beside Harold as he is informed of William's imminent arrival. Austin relates this directly to Harold's Yew. But these findings are hotly contested by English Heritage which owns the Battle site.

Austin equates another tree illustrated in the Bayeux Tapestry to the 'Hoary Apple Tree', which according to William of Poitiers account written c1075 is where the battle commenced. A nearby field is still known as 'Apple Tree Field'.

Then King William came from Normandy into Pevensey, on the eve of the Feast of St. Michael, and as soon as they were fit, made a castle at Hastings market-town. Then this became known to King Harold and he gathered a great raiding-army, and came against him at the hoary apple-tree. And William came upon him by surprise before his people were marshalled. Nevertheless the king fought very hard against him with those men who wanted to support him, and there was a great slaughter on either side. There were killed King Harold, and Earl Leofwine his brother, and Earl Gyrth his brother, and many good men. And the French had possession of the place of slaughter.

From *The Anglo-Saxon Chronicle*, 9th century.

ABOVE: The Bayeux Tapestry - Harold is informed of William's approach - yew tree to his right
OPPOSITE: Harold's Yew 2013

We pass to the Crowhurst Yew, growing in Crowhurst churchyard, close to the ruins of the Abbey, which, in Evelyn's time had a trunk ten feet in diameter. At the present day the trunk is hollow, but it still caries a noble and flourishing head.

From *A history of British forest trees* by John Selby 1842.

The Yew tree is without doubt a living link to the events of 1066. Estimates of its age range from 1,250-2,000 years. Split, hollow and sprawling across nearby gravestones, the tree has re-rooted where its branches meet the ground – an unusual sanction for a tree sited on ecclesiastical land, as they are usually 'tidied' by cutting any errant branches away. I measured the girth at 8.98m (29.46ft). In 1680 John Aubrey measured it at 8.2m (26.9ft), which means the trunk has only grown about 80cm (2.6ft) in 333 years – about 2.4mm a year – illustrating the slow growth and longevity of the species.

The name Crowhurst probably derives from the Anglo Saxon 'Crohha-hyrst' meaning 'muddy wooded hill'. In 1378 200 Oak trees were felled in the village to repair damage to fortifications in Rye suffered during the Hundred Years War.

In 1412, Henry IV awarded the manor to Sir John Pelham, who subsequently built the present day parish church, and probably planted the two other Yews which stand in the churchyard, themselves fine ancient specimens at 600 years old with girths of 5m (16.4ft).

Incidentally, if Harold really was killed by the infamous arrow in the eye, it was undoubtedly fired from a Norman bow, made of Yew.

ABOVE: The 'Younger' yew at Crowhurst 2013
BELOW: Crowhurst 1903 - Harold's Yew far left, large Oak in centre now lost

The Ninfield Yew
Ninfield, East Sussex

Preparing to meet the enemy, the king mounted the hill and strengthened both his wings with noble men. On the highest point of the summit he planted his banner, and ordered his other standards to be set up. All the men dismounted and left their horses in the rear, and taking their stand on foot they let the trumpets sound for battle

From *Carmen de Hastingae Proelio (Song of the Battle of Hastings)* attributed to Bishop Guy of Amiens c1067

ABOVE: The Ninfield Yew c1910
BELOW: The Ninfield Yew 2013

Once William had finished burning Crowhurst, he moved west to Ninfield, continuing his policy of laying waste to the Saxon manors. Like Crowhurst, Ninfield hosts an ancient Yew *(Taxus baccata)*. It is established in the churchyard of St Mary, where a church has stood since the eighth century.

It was here that William is said to have set his standard, and the hill on the high ground near the church still bears the name Standard Hill. On a good day, there are clear sight lines to the sea, a vantage point which would have offered the Saxons commanding views of William's impending approach.

In 1675, church records record the suicide of one Edward Cartwright, who hung himself from the tree. He was said to be the second person to have met his fate there, and was buried at a crossroads away from the church, a common practice for suicides in medieval times.

The circumference of 5.37 metres (17.6 feet) at ground level may belie the tree's true age. As can be seen from the photographs taken a century apart, the original outer shell has almost completely fallen away, some of it lost in the great storm of 1987. But re-growth in the form of new shoots within the trunk have given the tree its current shape, which closely follows its original character.

The Llangernyw Yew Conwy

In the churchyard of St Dygain's at Llangernyw stands one of the three oldest living trees in Wales – an ancient male Yew *(Taxus baccata)* with a girth of 10.36m (34ft) near the ground. At an estimated 3-4,000 years old, the tree predates the thirteenth century church by which it stands by several millennia, and together with The Defynnog and Discoed yews rivals the Fortingall Yew in Scotland as being the oldest living tree in northern Europe.

Originally the site was of circular shape before the church imposed its more rectangular boundaries, and standing in an elevated position, offered commanding panoramic views of the surrounding hills – prime location for a prehistoric Bronze Age sacred site. Two standing stones of at least Saxon antiquity stand on the south side of the church, absorbed along with the yew into the superseding Christian order – a principal long practised to ensure the smooth transition of the pagan populace to Christianity. However, accounts of village fairs taking place in the churchyard were reported as late as 1789, some 500 years after the ancient custom was outlawed.

Much of the trunk has long since decayed, and the tree now appears as four stems – each the size of a mature yew tree themselves. In fact, from the early 1990s until 1994 when Allen Meredith brought the tree to the world's attention in his Gazetteer of Ancient Yews, it had been used as a shelter for the church oil tank. It is thought that much old wood was removed in the process of installing the tank, making the accurate dating of the tree all the more complex.

A local woman had complained that one of the stems was leaning to such a degree that it made it difficult for her to visit a family grave, and her request that the branch be removed was granted. But on hearing of the historical significance of the tree, she agreed to move the gravestone instead. Her charitable action ensured the survival of the four remaining stems.

A tradition at Llangernyw echoes the pagan origins of the site, relating the tale of Angelystor, the recording angel, who revealed the names of the coming dead each All-Hallows Eve (Halloween).

On one such occasion, the local tailor, Nos G'lan Geua', or Shon Robert, as he was called, proceeded to the church to denounce the belief as fiction, only to hear his own name called out. He died before the year was through.

Shon Robert, as he was called, proceeded to the church just before midnight, and, to his horror, he heard his own name – "Shon ap Robert," uttered by the Spirit. "Hold, hold!" said the tailor, "I am not quite ready!"
But, ready or not ready, it made no difference to the messenger of death, for that year the tailor died.

From *Welsh Folk-Lore* by Elias Owen 1887

ABOVE: Lllangernyw Church c1920
BELOW AND OPPOSITE: The Llangernyw Yew 2012

The Pontfadog Oak
Pontfadog, Wrexham

The Pontfadog Oak in Wales (*Quercus petraea*) was the largest and oldest sessile oak in the country, and stood at a colossal 12.9m (42.3ft) in girth. It was a contender for the largest of its kind in the UK, and having lived for an estimated 1,200 years, was also one of the oldest.

When the tree first took root, Cynan Dindaethwy, King of Gwynedd, was fighting in vain to hold on to his kingdom. By 816 it had fallen into the hands of his brother Hywel, who deposed and exiled Cynan after a series of battles.

King Offa had built his famous Dyke – a 150 mile long ditch and bank territorial earthwork which ran 'from sea to sea', passing less than two miles east of Pontfadog. Following Offa's death in 796, Mercia briefly expanded into Gwynedd under the reign of Coenwulf, reducing Hywel's seat of power to Anglesey. It would not be not long though before Wessex became the dominant power under King Egbert, when he defeated Coenwulf's successor Beornwulf, in 825.

The Pontfadog Oak survived the felling of Ceiriog Woods in 1165 by Henry II's men, who were attempting to ease the passage of troops for Henry's attempted invasion of Wales. The English were ambushed by the Welsh hero Owain Gwynedd at the Battle of Crogen less than a mile away where they were defeated, heralding the end of Henry's offensive. Another ancient Oak (*Quercus robur*) measuring 9.61m (31.5ft), which recently split in two, marks the spot. It is known as 'The Oak at the Gate of the Dead', as the bodies of the fallen lie buried in the adjacent field, said never to have been shown a plough since.

Enduring the rise and fall of slate quarrying that operated in the Ceiriog Valley between 1329 and 1947, the long winter and prolonged snowfall of 2012 finally took its toll on The Pontfadog Oak, and it crashed down in a gale on 17th April 2013, revealing its shallow roots and ending its reign as Wales' oldest living Oak. The event created a sense of loss among many locals, so the owners decided to have part of the trunk carved into a lasting monument for the village. The Ancient Tree Forum managed to grow saplings from cuttings of the tree, so the gene pool lives on.

ABOVE: The Pontfadog Oak c1935

OPPOSITE: Once able to hold six persons within its hollow trunk 2012

BELOW: The fallen trunk of the Pontfadog Oak on 18th April 2013

*Unused as they are to battle.'
...in the great throne of battle
oak, the best, was exalted
before the other rulers...
The oak rushed
before him heaven and earth
trembled...*

From *Cad Goddeu (The Battle of the Trees)* Taliesin 14th C.

The Defynnog Yew
Defynnog, Powys

For centuries, a Yew tree *(Taxus baccata)* at Fortingall in Scotland was celebrated as being the oldest in Europe, thought to have lived for up to 5,000 years. In July 2014, several British national newspapers ran stories proclaiming a little known tree in Brecon, Wales, as a contender for the title.

At first sight, there appear to be four ancient Yew trees in St Cynog's churchyard – one 7.85m (25.75ft) girthed tree on the south side of the church, another 7.29m (24ft) on the east side, and two on the north-side – the first at 6.45m (21ft), beside the largest of the quartet which I found to measure 10.2m (33.46ft) in circumference at ground level.

Research conducted by Allen Meredith and Janis Fry led them to believe that the two Yews on the north-side could be one tree, and therefore much older than previously thought.

Twig samples tested by Roslin Forestry Research confirmed those suspicions when DNA from both trees was found to be an exact match. Meredith and Fry proposed that the two trunks are in fact one ancient tree that has split and grown apart, and suggested its age at upwards of 5,000 years. The Yew tree Campaign headed by David Bellamy supported the claim. In 1875 the then Lord Lieutenant of Brecon described 'one remarkable yew', and seen from above (right) the two trunks do appear to form one canopy.

There has been a church at Defynnog, founded by and since dedicated to St Cynog – eldest son of the warrior King of Brecon Brychan Brycheiniog – since around 473 AD. Cynog was martyred by marauding Saxons in 492 AD. The church houses a font carved with runic inscriptions dating from the Viking era, and an Ogam stone inscribed with a dedication to 'Rugniatis, son of Vendonius'.

The difficulty with dating European trees is their habit of losing heartwood as they decompose, making accurate dating by tree ring analysis impossible. For this reason some experts dispute Meridith and Fry's claims. The locale has been a sacred site since Neolithic times, and Meredith and Fry argue that the Yew was a sacred tree planted to commemorate a Bronze Age burial. If they are right, it means the Defynnog Yew has lived through at least five religions, and as many millennia.

Defynock which now contains one remarkable yew tree, as well as 2 other trees of the same kind, all walled round.

From notes made by Joseph Russell Bailey, Lord Lieutenant of Brecon 1875

ABOVE AND OPPOSITE: The Defynnog Yew 2014

BELOW LEFT: Roman stone in St Cynog's Church 2014

BELOW RIGHT: Viking Font St Cynog's Church 2014

Nordskoven Jaegerspris

Each war-ship, with its threatening throat
Of dragon fierce or ravenous brute
Grim gaping from the prow; its wales
Glittering with burnished shields, like scales
From *Heimskrinla* by Snorri Sturluson 1225

Nordskoven – the North Forest – sits on a north eastern peninsula of the island of Zealand, near the small town of Jaegerspris. A large remnant of native Danish woodland consisting mostly of Oak, Beech and Birch survives there. It was preserved as a royal hunting forest as early as the thirteenth century, when it was considerably larger; a playground for the Danish Kings who built an adjoining castle retreat to the south in Jaergerspris.

The area shows signs of being worked for timber since the Neolithic age, when wild boar, bear and wildcat roamed the forest. During Christian IV's reign (1588-1648), many oaks were felled for shipbuilding in Copenhagen, but in c1800 regulations were enforced to conserve and replant the forest. It continues to be used for forestry in parts laid out to more recent coniferous plantation, but the native forest has been protected since 1920.

It was from this part of the world that Viking warriors set off in search of trade and adventure in the ninth century, laying waste to large parts of Britain, northern Europe, Russia and the Baltic – lands they found easy prey, ripe for the taking.

They travelled by Longship – great sea-going warships driven by sail and oar that could carry up to 100 men. The craft were light and shallow enough to land directly on the beach, and could infiltrate the land via rivers and waterways, such was their manoeuvrability. They were constructed mainly from oak – hewn from Scandinavia's great forests – riveted together with iron.

In 1962, the remains of five boats were found at the bottom of Roskilde Fjord, just 10 km (6.2 miles) south east of Jaergerspris. Known as the Skuldelev

LEFT: Viking Longship from French Maritime League 1908
BELOW: Snoegen 2013

The North Forest is famed for three ancient Oaks; Storkeegen, the Stork Oak – named after a breeding pair of Storks that once nested in its branches – has a girth of 10.15m (34.4ft). It died in 1981, its crown torn off in a hurricane. The rotting, cave-like hulk is a reminder of its former splendour. Nearby stand the remains of Snoegen – the Twisted Oak – with a girth of around 9m (29.5ft). Dead since 1991, it resembles a ghost-like sculpture; twisted body, arms flailing, and plays host to a huge colony of wood ants. Its twisted trunk probably saved it from the axe.

Large Beech trees (*Fagus sylvatica*) are also common in the forest, I measured several at over 5m (16.4ft) in circumference. Nordskoven's pièce de résistance however, the largest of the trio and Denmark's oldest tree, is the great Kongeegen.

ABOVE LEFT: Storkeegen 1914

BELOW: Storkeegen 2013

Ships; two Longships, two trading ships and one fishing vessel were tied together, filled with stones and deliberately sunk, the whole structure forming a barricade. It seems that although the Viking raiding parties were playing away on organised raids, their rapine appetite was also voracious on the home front.

Carbon dating and dendrochronolgy – the analysis of tree rings – found the ships' timbers to date between 1030 and 1040. The flotilla was sunk in the 1060s to protect Denmark's then capital, Roskilde, and could have been a reaction to King Harald Harada's ravaging of the Danish coast in 1064, two years before he was defeated by Harold Godwinson at the Battle of Stamford Bridge in England in 1066. The largest of the five ships was found to have been constructed in Dublin from Irish oak, the smaller Longship and trader however were made of oak felled from eastern Denmark.

In 1997, whilst constructing the Viking Ship Museum to display the ships, excavation uncovered nine further vessels, including Roskilde 6 – at 32m (105ft), the longest Viking ship ever found, built sometime after 1025 from Danish Oak.

Kongeegen Nordskoven Jaegerspris

Kongeegen – The King's Oak – was named after King Frederick VII who purchased Jaegerspris Castle – long the haunt of Danish Kings – for himself in 1854.

Official estimates put the Pendunculate Oak *(Quercus robur)*, at between 1400-1900 years old, which means that the tree has not only outlived Frederick, but predates him and all the kings of the Viking age (c800-1100) by several centuries. Kongeegen stood as a substantial landmark tree throughout the time of the early Vikings, who associated Oaks with Thor, god of thunder, as the tree was often seen to be struck by lightning. As a consequence, lone acorns were sometimes kept on windowsills to protect homes from lightning strikes.

Standing only 150m (500ft) from the bank of Roskilde Fjord, Kongeegen bore witness to the comings and goings of the longships as they travelled to and fro, visible across the marshland that separates the forest from the water. Curiously, the oak was rediscovered only as recently as 1842 by local foresters.

I measured the girth of the tree at 10.3m (33.8ft) at 1m (3.3ft) from the ground. Large parts of the trunk have collapsed, and its primary branch fell in 1973, itself the size of a mature Oak tree. I would guess that in its prime the trunk once doubled my measurement. A ring of stones is laid out to mark its likely former size.

The tree still carries a vigorous crown – no acorns were evident on my mid-September visit – but ancient oaks may only fruit occasionally, especially when they reach this grand old age.

Kongeegen is fenced off for its own protection, whilst the Nordskoven is left seemingly to its own devices, gradually turning to wildwood. The great Oak has seen the forest change over millennia, is the elder statesman of its species in Scandinavia, and a contender for one of Europe's oldest Oaks.

He who stood a rooted oak,
Unshaken by the swordsman's stroke,
Amidst the whiz of arrows slain,
Has fallen upon Fjalar's plain.
From *Heimskrinla* by Snorri Sturluson 1225

ABOVE: Kongeegen c1905
OPPOSITE: Kongeegen 2013

Dyrehaven
Jaegersborg

Just 10km (6 miles) north of Copenhagen sits Jaegersborg Dyrehave, a deer park which covers almost 10km² (6miles²). It is home to around 2,100 deer, and is one of Denmark's most visited sites, attracting over 2 million visitors a year since it was opened to the public in 1756.

Anciently known as Boveskov (Beech Wood), the area was first enclosed by King Frederick III as a royal hunting forest – his only private deer park – in 1669. Red deer were driven into the fenced area where they could be contained and hunted at the King's leisure.

The Dyrehaven hosts as many as 1,000 ancient or veteran Oak and Beech trees, with areas of Alder, Field Maple and Hawthorn. When they die, the trees are left to lie where they fall, and are only removed if deemed a danger to the public, thereby providing a habitat for a myriad of creatures and fungi, many of which live only in this particular environment. Fallen Beech trees are particularly common in the south of the park where the tree density is higher, and litter the floor in places like fallen sculptures. One of the largest pasture woodland sites in Northern Europe, grassland and sapling grazing by the deer allows the ancient oak and beech trees space to grow, affording them the light they need to thrive. The number of deer is kept to around 2,100; any more and the land becomes over-grazed, any less and the trees are smothered by new growth, so around 700 adult deer are culled every year, equalling the amount of calves born each summer, retaining the current landscape.

Frederick's son; Christian V, expanded on his father's plans and enlarged the forest considerably

Sigurd, who once on Hadding's grave
A feast to Odin's ravens gave.

From *Heimskrinla* by Snorri Sturluson 1225

Above: Ravneeg 2013

to allow him the space required for hunting with dogs, a practice he learned from the French court whilst visiting Louis XIV. It involves chasing a stag with dogs until it falls from exhaustion. It is then killed with a knife by a senior member of the hunt, a practice remembered at the Christian V Oak in the north of the park – an ancient Oak named after the time the King finished a hapless beast with his own Hirsch Piper – a royal dagger.

On my visit, I entered the Dyrehaven from the south near the Bakken, the oldest amusement park in the world created 400 years ago. I was searching for Ravneeg, an ancient, hollow, pollard Oak 5.3m (17.3ft) in circumference, named after the Ravens that still frequent the Dyrehaven. Ravens feature prominently in Norse mythology. Huginn and Muninn – the primary god Odin's pair of Ravens – would fly out each day and return to inform him of all that had gone on in the world. The Vikings often portrayed images of the bird on flags, banners and shields, and would release them on longship voyages to find new lands. If the bird returned, they knew they were far from land, but if it flew ahead,

ABOVE: Hjorte Kilde Oak 2013
LEFT: Decaying Beech trunk 2013

and did not return, they would follow its direction. The Norse sagas describe this as the means by which the Vikings discovered Iceland.

I walked the path adjacent to the northern limit of Klampenborg Galopbane – the adjacent racecourse – to find Raven Oak. I could hear the galloping feet of horses as they raced the course, and was shocked to see an entire race, led by a riderless horse, leave the course and head straight towards me at full gallop as they followed the leader along a sandy exit track. I looked on in disbelief as the leading horse ran straight into the six foot metal gates that barred the exit. The locked gates burst open, relieved from their hinges. The adrenalin-pumped horse, having fallen badly, was writhing on the ground. It then leapt to its feet and disappeared at speed into the forest, narrowly avoiding a couple and their child.

In 1763, the botanist Johann Georg von Langen took the initiative to replant the Dyrehaven, notably at Von Langens Plantation in the south east of the park which is named after him, and contains many mature trees now 250 years old.

Ulvesdal Oak   Jaegersborg Dyrehaven

As well as the aforementioned named Oaks, the park hosts over a dozen other ancients, most of which have lived upwards of 400 years.

Of these, the largest, oldest and most impressive is undoubtedly Ulvesdal's eg (Wolf Valley Oak). Named after the glacier-formed valley in which it sits, the Pedunculate Oak *(Quercus robur)* stands alone in a large clearing at the bottom of Djævlebakken (Devils Hill), Dyrehaven's highest point and favourite toboggan run. The hill is fringed by the forms of ancient, twisted Beech trees. The Oak has long outlived the wolves that once roamed here. Estimates of its age range from 600-1,000 years, suggesting it was planted towards the end of the Viking era. I measured its split, hollow crumbling trunk at a colossal 10.95m (35.9ft), making it the second fattest Oak in Denmark after Kongeegen, and possibly the second oldest, but the tree still supports a voluminous crown which on my visit was packed with large, healthy acorns, and the trunk naturally appears to have many faces, as if sculpted into its decaying wood.

An open air theatre; Ulvedalsteateret, has been held sporadically beside the Oak during the summer months. The very first performance in 1910 was Hagbart and Signe by Adam Oehlenschläger, the Danish poet and playwright who wrote Denmark's national anthem. He is said to have carved his name on an ancient Oak tree at the Dyrehaven whilst there.

Nearby at Klampenborg station stands the Park's second oldest Oak, Skovfogedeg (Forester Oak), planted over 800 years ago with a girth of 10.45m (34.28ft). It was named after a Catholic forester who would visit its cavernous, hollow trunk to pray.

LEFT AND OPPOSITE:
Ulvesdal Oak 2013

The Kvilleken   Norra Kvill

In southern Sweden near Norra Kvill National Park, at the Oaks' northernmost range in Europe, stands the country's oldest tree. Known as the Kvilleken, the tree also holds the record as Europe's largest girthed Oak (*Quercus robur*).

   The Kvilleken's first mention appears in 1772 when Magnus Gabriel Craelius described it in his 'Essay in the Description of a Landscape' as a tool shed used by local farmers. Craelius found it measured 13.06m (42.65ft) in circumference. By 1926 it had reached 13.36m (43.8ft). Today, it stands at a colossal 15.1m (49.5ft) around its hollow bole, reaching the same measurement in height.

   Estimated to be 1,000 years old, it is a wonder that the tree survived at all. Oaks are unusually susceptible to lightning strike, and for that reason are associated in Norse mythology with Thor, the god of thunder. This recalls the tale of Volsung (the great grandson of Odin, father of the gods) and his Great Hall, which was supported by a great Oak. At the wedding of Volsung's daughter Signy, Odin appeared and set a challenge for all attending. He thrust into Volsung's Oak a magic sword that bestowed undefeatable power to the wielder and proclaimed that the person who could pull it out would keep it. The sword was won by Volsung's son Sigmund. Volsung's jealous son-in-law Siggeur set a trap for him and his ten sons and bound them to a tree where Siggeur's mother changed into a wolf and ate them all. Only Sigmund survived and – aptly – exacted his revenge using the magic sword.

   In 1746 a law was passed declaring Swedish Oaks property of the state, such was the demand for their timber for house and ship building. Lasting 130 years, the act did nothing to help the cause of Oak preservation, causing resentment amongst landowners, and the Oak's population declined further.

   By the 1960s, retrenchment, hollowing and decay had reached such an extent that a local blacksmith was hired to fix a supportive metal band around the tree to help prevent collapse. In July 2005, the band was removed by a man claiming that the Oak could no longer breathe. To some extent he was right, as the metal had become deeply embedded and was inhibiting cambial growth. Earlier that year, Kvilleken had withstood the might of hurricane Gudrun, which brought down many thousands of trees in Sweden.

   Following assessment support was deemed necessary, so a system of 16 stainless steel bolts supporting a tensioned steel cable was fitted in 2013, it will hopefully prolong the Kvilleken's longevity.

ABOVE: The Kvilleken 1926

BELOW AND OPPOSITE: The Kvilleken 2010

Within 150 years of the famous Black Death, the biggest oaks in this resort first flowed up out of the earth, one that is still fresh and stands on the Lieutnant's Bostället Norra Qvills lands, is remarkable because it is 22 cubits around the torso; she is now hollow; and I have myself climbed, stood inside her; farmers on Bostället use her as a tool shed.

From *Försök till ett landskaps beskrivning* by Magnus Gabriel Craelius 1772

Chène Chapelle
Allouville Bellefosse, Normandy

In the central northern French village of Allouville Bellefosse stands Chène Chapelle, the Chapel Oak *(Quercus robur)*, sometimes quoted as the oldest in France. Local tradition attributes an age of at least 1,000 years to the Oak, and tells how William of Normandy knelt at the base of the tree as a young boy in 1035, some 31 years before his venture to England procured him the English throne following his victory at the Battle of Hastings.

Experts are less generous with their estimates, proposing an age of only 800 years, but with a girth of 15m (49ft) at its base, it is possible that the tree is as old as folklore suggests. This latter judgement places the tree as a sapling in the thirteenth century at the time of Philip II Augustus, first King of France, who reigned from 1190 until his death in 1223.

In 1696 the Chapel Oak was struck by lightning, causing the tree to catch fire and hollowing its trunk in the process. The Oak not only survived but blossomed following the trauma. Deemed a miracle by the local pastor Abbot Du Détroit and village priest Father Du Cerceau, they dedicated the tree to the Virgin Mary, building an altar within the hollow and naming it Notre Dame de la Paix (Our Lady of Peace). Later a second chapel, Chambre de l'Ermite (the Hermit's Room) was constructed, along with a spiral staircase leading to it.

Almost a century later during the French Revolution in 1793, the tree escaped calamity again when having fired an ancient Beech and Blackthorn tree in the vicinity, a mob of revolutionaries, blind with fury, set upon the Oak as a symbol of authority, the church and the old ways. The Village Schoolmaster Jean-Baptiste Bonheur had the bright idea of hanging a sign on the trunk declaring it

'temple of reason', which had the effect of calming the crowd and saving the tree.

In 1887 villagers restored the chapel with internal Oak panelling and hundreds of wooden shingles where the bark had fallen away. A century on saw further restoration and the use both internally and externally of a complex structure of metal props to support the tree. Both restorations reflecting technologies of their time.

The Chapel Oak may today seem to be more at home in a theme park, but it is the very act of it becoming firstly a chapel and then a tourist attraction that has given the tree such longevity. I saw no other trees of note in the area, just mile upon mile of flat earth given over to the plough. Any other notable siblings have long been lost to the axe. Twice a year mass is still held inside its bole, and on August 15 each year, an annual pilgrimage celebrating the Feast of the Assumption of the Virgin takes place there.

Although the Chapel Oak may seem to be on its last legs, unallowed to grow old and decay naturally, its surviving branches still offer a glorious leafy crown and a broad crop of acorns in the autumn.

ABOVE LEFT: Chène Chapelle by Jules Janin 1844

LEFT: Chène Chapelle c1910

RIGHT: Chène Chapelle 2009

The Robin Locust Paris

Paris can boast many remarkable trees, notably at the Jardin des Plantes, but the city's oldest tree can be found across the water from the Cathedral of Notre Dame, near the left bank of the River Seine, in René Viviani Montebello Square, beside Saint Julien le Pauvre church.

A Black Locust or False Acacia tree, it was planted in 1601 by Jean Robin (1550-1629), gardener to King Henry IV. Robin grew seeds imported from eastern North America where the tree is native, and is remembered in its scientific name *(Robinia pseudoacacia)*. He was responsible for introducing the species to Europe, and it thrives widely on the continent.

The tree stands 11m (36ft) tall and has a circumference of 3.5m (11.5ft). The deeply furrowed, hollow trunk leans at an acute angle, as it has done for at least a century, and is now supported by two concrete columns, disguised in some part by the ivy that clings to the tree.

The square has held religious significance for many centuries. A Merovingian basilica and cemetery dating from the 6th-century predate the current church, itself one of the oldest monastic buildings in Paris, constructed between 1165 and 1250. During the French revolution (1789–1799), the building narrowly avoided demolition, which would no doubt have necessitated the demise of the tree, and was renovated in the mid-nineteenth century. It is positioned at the apex of two important ancient roads leading from Spain and Italy respectively.

During the First World War, the Locust tree suffered a blow from a shell, losing its upper branches in the process. But it survived the attack and has continued to blossom each summer, yielding fragrant, creamy white flowers in pendulous droplets.

Often overlooked in the busy square, the tree is supported by a concrete column, sculpted to resemble a tree trunk, surrounded by a circular bench set above a latticed framework hand-woven from Chestnut wands. I found it a perfect place to take respite from the ravages of the city.

The trees that are slow to grow bear the best fruit.
Quote from Molière 1622-1673.

ABOVE: The Robin Locust c1910
OPPOSITE: The Robin Locust, with Notre Dame visible beyond 2013

Fontainebleau Forest
Centre

Situated about 35 miles (5km) south of Paris, the Fontainebleau Forest stretches over some 85 square miles (220 square km). It has been a Royal hunting forest since the middle of the twelfth century when Louis VII built a lodge and chapel there, at least 34 sovereigns have subsequently spent time there. Famously, Napoleon Bonaparte waved an emotional goodbye to his troops at Fontainebleau from whence he was exiled to the island of Elba in 1814.

The forest cover is mostly Oak (44%), interspersed with areas of Beech, Birch and the non-native Scots Pine. The rare endemic tree, Alisier de Fontainebleau *(Sorbus latifolia)*, a Whitebeam hybrid, is protected by the Office National des Forêts, as is the rest of the forest.

Veteran trees, remnants of a time when cattle grazed beneath them creating pasture woodland, offer a landscape reminiscent of many in Europe, but grazing stopped in the early eighteenth century, leaving large areas the chance to re-grow. While both deer and wild boar roam freely, some of the veteran trees now struggle for light amongst the overgrowth.

Trees and heather grow on sandy soil amongst an array of seemingly random boulders, some bearing ancient prehistoric carvings. The oldest date back to 8000 BC, providing evidence of human habitation here during the Mesolithic period.

Between the 1820s and 1870s, a new school of artists set themselves up in the village of Barbizon, venturing into the forest to capture its natural beauty. Amongst them Théodore Rousseau (1812–1867), Jean-François Millet (1814–1875) and Claude Monet (1840–1926), paved the way for impressionism. Writers and poets followed, including Robert Louis Stevenson, who wrote his 'Forest Notes' at Barbizon in 1876. The lodgings in which he stayed still bear his name.

One day, in the sixteenth century, St Louis was hunting in the forest of Bieve, in the Gatinais. He lost a dog he was very fond of, and which answered to the name of Bleau. The king was very much vexed at his loss, and all the court exerted themselves to recover it. Saints as well as other beings have all their flatterers. The flatterers of St Louis hurried so swiftly about the forest, that they found the dog drinking at a spring. The spring was made into a fountain, which was called Fontainebleau.

From *The Illustrated Magazine of Art* 1854

ABOVE: Veteran Fontainebleau Oak amongst the ferns 2013

ABOVE: Veteran Oak near Barbizon 1902

Sandstone was previously quarried here to build houses in Paris and metal the roads, easily transported to the city via the River Seine, which meanders through the north east of the forest. Areas of timber plantation still occur, with evidence of clear felling in places, and while recreation and tourism are Fontainebleau's primary contemporary use, it can still lay claim to being a working woodland, a practice set to increase in the future and enlarge the footprint of the forest.

Comely beeches send up their white, straight, clustered branches, barred with green moss, like so many fingers from a half-clenched hand. Mighty oaks stand to the ankles in a fine tracery of underwood; thence the tall shaft climbs upwards, and the great forest of stalwart boughs spreads out into the golden evening sky, where the rooks are flying and calling.

From *Forest Notes* by Robert Louis Stevenson 1876

ABOVE: Veteran 'Screaming' Beech amongst the boulders 2013

61

Under this oak-tree is pleasanter on such a day than in my cabinet. Seat yourself there, my trusty councillor, on that wooden seat, and let us talk of affairs of state.

Henry IV to Sully, from '*The Oak of Henry IV at Fontainebleau*', *Illustrated Magazine of Art* 1854

The Sully Oak
Fontainebleau Forest

Duc de Sully, the Duke of Sully (1560-1641), was Henry IV's right hand man, appointed finance minister following the Wars of Religion, and partly responsible for twenty years of relative peace and economic stability thereafter.

A lesser known fact in the annals of history is Sully's passion for trees. He forbade destruction of the forests, a practice that was fast gathering pace, and ordered the planting of trees, a point reflected in the many ancient trees named after him across France. He initiated the practice of planting avenues of roadside Poplars and village Plane trees, but planted mostly Elms – valued for the production of gun carriages.

At Fontainebleau, an avenue running south of the Gorges Apremont bears his name; Route de Sully, and runs through the forest for around 2 miles (3 km). It is notable for two large Sessile Oaks (*Quercus petraea*), which stand either side of the track, about 250m (820ft) apart.

The larger of the pair with a girth of 5.08m (16.6ft), is the named tree, and stands beside a sign proclaiming it 'Chêne Sully' - Sully's Oak. But the smaller tree, measuring 4.67m (15.32ft) in circumference, fenced off but unsigned, bears more than a passing resemblance to the Sully Oak photographed extensively for postcards a century or so ago, unlike the named tree.

Sully may not have planted these trees himself, but they were surely planted under his decree. There is no doubt that he spent time here – a painting made between 1783 and 1787 by François-André Vincent; 'Henri IV et Sully à Fontainebleau' illustrates Sully at Henry IV's feet in the forest, and now hangs in the Château at Fontainebleau.

These are some of the few veteran Oaks remaining in the forest, struggling to hold their own amongst the secondary growth that threatens to engulf them. Oaks are light loving trees, and need space in which to thrive.

ABOVE: The Sully Oak c1920
OPPOSITE: The Sully Oak 2013
BELOW: The original Sully Oak? 2013

The Charlemagne Oak
Fontainebleau Forest

Chêne Charlemagne - Charlemagne's Oak - may be a less impressive example of the named trees in Fontainebleau forest in terms of age and girth at only 3.04m (10ft), but the Sessile Oak *(Quercus petraea)* certainly impresses in height.

It stands on the Route des Mazettes – once the main route into the forest from Barbizon – and was planted in 1802 along with many other Oaks. It is the close planting of the trees that caused them to grow tall rather than wide. When the plantation was thinned, this tree was spared as the best of the crop, and named in 2000 by local school children after Charlemagne (742-814), King of the Franks and Holy Roman Emperor. It is now surrounded by young Beech trees.

Previously, there stood a pair of Oaks 'Le Charlemagne et le Roland', commemorating 'the father of Europe' and his legendary paladin at Mont Ussy due north of Fontainebleau town, but they are both lost. Charlemagne and Roland are dead – long live Charlemagne.

Above: Le Charlemagne et le Roland c1905
Right: Charlemagne's Oak 2013

64

The Jupiter Oak
Fontainebleau Forest

Just 2 miles (3 km) west of Fontainebleau town stands the oldest and largest tree in the forest, Chêne Jupiter – the Jupiter Oak, named after the Roman King of the Gods, whose sacred tree was the Oak. A tall, straight Sessile Oak *(Quercus petraea)*, it measures 6.25m (20.5ft) in circumference, even without bark, and is thought to be upwards of 600 years old.

One hundred years ago, the tree was a well-visited tourist attraction accompanied by stalls, shelters and signposts, as evidenced by the archive photograph below.

Jupiter died in the summer of 1994, after three years of drought, but still stands tall – an organic, natural sculpture – host to myriad life forms, of which the Oak supports more than any other tree in the forest. The Office National des Forêts has done well to let him grow old gracefully.

ABOVE: The Jupiter Oak c1900
RIGHT: The Jupiter Oak 2013

Bouquet de la Reine Amélie
Fontainebleau Forest

Just north of Fontainebleau at the top of a high escarpment overlooking the town, stands a large Sessile Oak (*Quercus petraea*), with a girth of 4.25m (13.9ft) at 1.1m (3.6ft) from the ground.

Known as Bouquet de la Reine Amélie, the tree was named in honour of France's last Queen. Born in Naples, daughter of Ferdinand I King of the Two Sicilies, Marie-Amélie married Louis-Philippe who became King of France in 1830 following the July Revolution.

Marie-Amélie took little interest in politics, as she feared further revolution – possibly instilled by the execution of her aunt Marie Antoinette by guillotine following the first dissolution of the monarchy in 1792. She dedicated herself to family life, and witnessed Louis-Philippe's extravagant restoration and embellishment of the Royal Palace at Fontainebleau. He also continued Napoleon's efforts to replant 2,428ha (6,000ac) of forest.

Marie-Amélie's fears were realised however when the revolution of 1848 forced Louis-Philippe to abdicate, and the couple fled to England where they spent the rest of their lives. Louis-Philippe died only two years later in 1850, but Marie-Amélie lived until 1866, aged 88.

The tree is reached via paths from the Route de la Reine Amelie, a winding trail that leads from Fontainebleau town high into the forest. On the way you pass a bust dedicated to Nemorosa, Queen of the Forest, fixed to a large sandstone boulder. Sculpted by Adam Solomon in 1948, it remembers a tale of the French knight, René de Fontainebleau, who hid his beautiful lover Delia in a cave in the wood in 1346 to keep her from danger, whilst the town of Samois was being held to siege by the Black Prince. On his return, René found his lover lifeless, killed by a viper. He sat on a rock, and cried uncontrollably in grief. That night, Nemorosa appeared, crowned with flowers, and consoled him. A new love was formed, and the pair ascended to heaven, where they could be together forever.

In the Queen's bed-chamber are many royal ladies. Marie de Medici, Marie-Therese, Marie-Antoinette, Marie-Louise, wife of Napoleon, and Marie-Amelie of Louis-Philippe, have entitled it to be called the "Chambre des cinq Maries."
From '*Fontainebleau*' The Brisbane Courier 1930

ABOVE: Queen Marie-Amélie 1860
BELOW: Nemorosa, Reine de Bois monument 2013
OPPOSITE: Bouquet de la Reine Amélie 2013

Joan of Arc's Lime Vaucouleurs

In February 1429, Joan of Arc arrived in Vaucouleurs from her family home in Domrémy 12 miles (19.5km) to the south. She had come to petition Robert de Baudricourt for an audience with King Charles VII, her only route to gain official support for her quest to rid France of the English, and restore the country to French rule.

Joan had had a vision beneath a sacred Beech tree in the woods at Domrémy, where an angel came to her and explained what she must do. On arrival at Vaucouleurs, legend has Joan tethering her horse to a Lime tree at the Porte de France, where she rested beneath its leafy shade beside a church where she later prayed. The Lime tree *(Tilia x europaea)* still stands, and is now a classified historical monument, all of 600 years old. It is rooted at two levels – above and below the castle embankment – and measures 7.7m (25.2ft) above and 3.6m (11.8ft) below the revetment. The hollow trunk, long bricked up and filled with cement, provides a home for a myriad of creatures including birds, beetles and other invertebrates and a colony of black ants who have constructed their nest where the trunk meets the revetment wall. Bees buzz busily in the dense canopy, intoxicated by the sweet aroma of the Lime flowers.

After three attempts to petition Baudricourt – who was initially incredulous that a woman could take on the might of the English where he had failed – Joan was eventually accepted and gained the support of the King. The fact that she ultimately failed in her task is no measure of her dedication and bravery. Joan won many victories in battle, and it was only betrayal by Burgundian officals – her fellow countrymen – that handed her to the English, whose response to the considerable thorn in their side was to burn her at the stake on 30th May 1431, aged just nineteen.

Her final words *"My Voices did come from God and everything that I have done was by God's order"* reflect her strength and dedication to her cause. The fact that she was posthumously canonised by the Catholic Church in 1920 goes some way to redressing the balance in her favour.

...near Domrémy, there was a certain tree called the Ladies' Tree, and others called it the Fairies' Tree; and near by is a fountain. And she has heard that people sick of the fever drink of this fountain and seek its water to restore their health; It is a big tree, a beech, from which they get the fair May, in French le beau may; ... and often she had heard the old folk say (not those of her family) that the fairies frequented it.

Asked if the saints spoke to her at the fountain near the tree, she answered yes, she heard them there, ...the voice told her that she, Jeanne, should go to Robert de Baudricourt, in the town of Vaucouleurs of which he was captain, and he would provide an escort for her...Robert twice refused to hear her and repulsed her; the third time he listened to her and gave her an escort. And the voice had told her that it would be so.

From *The Trial of Jeanne d'Arc* translated by W P Barrett 1903

ABOVE: Joan of Arc's Lime tree at Vaucouleurs 1900
OPPOSITE: Joan of Arc's Lime tree at Vaucouleurs 2013

Hohle Eiche
Rellingen, Schleswig-Holstein

In the town of Rellingen, 19km (11.8 miles) north west of central Hamburg, stands an ancient oak *(Quercus robur)* known as Hohle Eiche, the Hollow Oak, in a street named Hohle Eiche, and hollow indeed it is, as it has been for centuries.

Measured at 8.5m (27.8ft) in 2000, the tree ranks as the 37th largest girthed Oak in Germany according to the German Tree Archive, but my measurement of 9.17m (30ft) at 1.3m taken in 2014 would place it squarely in the top 20.

When the archive photograph (opposite) was taken by local photographer Hermann Möller in 1910, the more complete trunk measured 10m (32.8ft), which would raise it to a top 10 position. Amongst the nine men pictured, Möller's photograph identifies seven local men: Hermann Behrens, Claus Hatje, Ernst Timm – innkeeper of the Hollow Oak Inn – now gone, Rudolf Hatje, Ernst Timms Schwager and Franz Hatje. At this time a table and chairs graced the hollow trunk, which could comfortably seat four people. In 1942 the Inn was used to house Rellingen's volunteer fire department, but was moved to a new station after World War II.

Fittingly known for its tree nurseries which replaced traditional agricultural lands, Rellingen previously hosted large tracts of woodland, but most of these were lost following the hardships of the Second World War. The Hohle Eiche is almost certainly a woodland pasture remnant, typical of northern Europe.

In 2007 a decision was taken to reduce the crown of the tree, as steel cables fitted to support its branches were torn from the tree and it was deemed unsafe.

Registered as a natural monument, official estimates put the Oak at 500-600 years old, but the people of Rellingen proudly proclaim it a Tausendjährige Eiche; a Thousand Year Oak, and when compared to other trees held to be that age, I see no reason to differ.

Refreshing shade you grant us, venerable oak!
  From the inside hollowed, age ate your core;
Strength failed you indeed, but you break the fury of
    the storm;
  A picture of the constitution of the kingdom,
    which also had to fall!

From *Die Hohle Eiche* by Ludwig von Bayern 1830

ABOVE: The Hohle Eiche 2014
OPPOSITE: The Hohle Eiche c1910

71

The Jenischpark Oak Hamburg

To the west of Hamburg city centre on the north bank of the River Elbe sits Jenischpark, a 43ha (110ac) protected area – Hamburg's oldest landscaped park.

It was created as a model ornamental farm and arboretum in an English garden style between 1785-1800 for Caspar Voght (1752-1839), a successful German merchant largely remembered for reforming Hamburg's welfare system. In his later years he grew tired of business, handed most of his affairs to his American partner, and concentrated on his passion for horticulture.

In 1828 Voght sold the park to his friend Hamburg banker and Senator Martin Jenisch (1760-1827), and it was remodelled in his name, without agricultural purpose. Jenisch also had a summer house built which remained in family hands for a century. Today the house hosts a museum dedicated to upper-class 19th century life, offering an insight into Jenisch's world.

The park was finally purchased by the City of Hamburg in 1939 and remains open to the public.

As well as the Beech, Sweet Chestnuts and other trees planted during its creation, the park also hosts a collection of ancient Oak *(Quercus robur)* wood pasture, some examples of which predate its inception. Several measure around 5m (16.4ft) in girth, but the largest, a sprawling hollow Oak 7.83m (25.6ft) in circumference could be over 400 years old. The large opening is bound together in the curious German tradition of inserting iron bars, which have the effect of resembling a step-ladder – an ideal climbing aid for inquisitive children, whilst acting as a deterrent to keep larger animals (and adults) out. I spotted several old Oaks there that had received the same treatment.

On my visit the Oak had a bed of hay laid on the floor of its cavernous bole, and a local family took shelter beneath its flourishing boughs – the perfect spot for a picnic.

Mr. V. had been invited by the Emperor to Vienna, where he has been for some months engaged... in forming & establishing a plan for... the Promotion of Industry & the improvement of the condition of the lower orders, on the principles of the Hamburgh Reform. An account of this last has been printed & published at Vienna at the Emperor's request & expense.

William Wilberforce in a letter to Rev Wellbeloved 1802

ABOVE: Jenisch House and Oak c1935
OPPOSITE: The Oldest Oak in Jenischpark 2014

Hasbruch Forest

Lower Saxony

In northern Germany close to Bremen, stand 630 ha (1,557ac) of ancient forest known as 'Das Hasbrucher Urwald' – the Hasbruch Virgin Forest – but while it may appear to be overgrown and wild, the description is somewhat misleading.

Virgin forest conjures an image of untouched primeval jungle, but Hasbruch is a remnant of a once much larger area of Oak woodland with a long history shaped by its people since the Stone Age.

Teutonic tribes may well have worshipped their sacred Oak groves here, and bronze age burial mounds at nearby Stenum provide clear evidence of early habitation. But the 'thousand year Oaks' that punctuate the woodland are survivors of the classic medieval wood-pasture system so often witnessed across northern Europe. From Britain to Romania and beyond, scattered relics of a feudal landscape accorded the light-loving Oaks the space they required to thrive. Spared competition from other trees by grazing animals which kept competition at bay by eating the succulent young saplings, these

A friend of the soul, a physician of the body, a blessing of our donors fields - what could be said of all forests - these are general things the members of every other nation understands. But the bond which connects the German with his forest is much narrower - it winds itself into the depths of thought and feeling and is inherited from generation to generation; because the history of his people is linked everywhere in the forest.

From *Der Hasbruch Ein Deutsches Waldbild* by Ferdinand Lindner 1880

ABOVE: Hasbruch Forest by Ferdinand Lindner 1880
LEFT: German Pagan Oak Cult c1914

were primarily working forests of Oak, Beech and Hornbeam, providing firewood and fencing by pollarding, food and habitat for grazers and a semi-open landscape enabling the feudal masters to hunt. In 1258 the forest was noted as belonging to Hude Monastery, and afforded it grazing rights.

In 1578 several thousand swine were recorded in the forest, benefitting from mast-rights which gave permission to fatten them on the acorns of the forest floor, confirming the prolifacy of Oak.

Around 1740 the last wolf in the area was shot. Ten years later only 1,000 swine are recorded. But by 1800, uncontrolled grazing had left large parts of Hasbruch open and bare, and efforts were put in place to protect it. By 1850, parts of the forest were excluded from grazing, and left to revert to their wild state. In this period, tracks were laid to work the forest which accommodated a growing number of visitors, reflecting the romantic attitudes towards ancient Oaks that prevailed at the time.

However, large parts of Hasbruch were still harvested for timber. Between 1945-46 many trees were felled to help with reconstruction after the war, further reducing its size, but since 1997, the forest has been designated as a nature reserve.

A visit to Hasbruch today presents a thick, wild wood, bursting with life from dung-beetle to giant Oak; but the decision to leave the forest to its own devices is having a detrimental effect on the remaining ancient Oaks. Beech trees are becoming dominant, over-shading the old pollard Oaks and Hornbeams, causing them to reduce further still, while the dense canopy makes regeneration of new Oaks all the more difficult as sunlight struggles to reach the forest floor.

ABOVE: Charlotteneiche 1916

LEFT: Hasbruch Forest Beech Avenue 2014

The official map of Hasbruch forest shows just sixteen named and notable Oaks, many of which are in decline, and some of which are fallen. For example, nothing remains of the Charlotte Oak (above) – named after Sophie Charlotte (1879-1964), daughter of the Grand Duke Friederich of Oldenburg – once the subject of photographs and postcards produced to whet the appetites of early twentieth century romantics.

The Amalien Oak
Hasbruch Forest

The undisputed champion, King of Hasbruch Forest's 'thousand year Oaks' was the aptly named Dicke Eiche; the Thick Oak, with a noted girth of 11m (36ft). But at 4pm on Sunday 8 July 1923, forest rangers spotted smoke coming from the tree. By 5pm the trunk was engulfed in flames, past saving, and collapsed shortly after 8pm.

It appears that a gymnastic club had climbed the tree, ignoring signs to keep off, and tossed a lit cigarette butt into the hollow trunk as they left. Almost a century later, remains of the fallen trunk are still clearly visible.

A new champion took the mantle in the form of the Amalien Oak, a 10m (32.8ft) girthed giant. The tree was named after Augustus, Grand Duke of Oldenburg's first daughter, Princess Amalie (1818-1875), who became Queen consort of Greece when she married King Otto (1815–1867), aged just 19. At first Greece took her to its heart, but she later fell victim to harsh attacks, surviving an assassination attempt in 1861. It is thought that the Queen's unpopularity was due in part to her inability to provide an heir. The following year, after an uprising in Athens, the Royal couple fled on board a British warship bound for Bavaria where they lived out the rest of their days in exile.

Around the time of Amalie's marriage, artists began pilgrimages to Hasbruch, sketching and painting the great Oaks, staying in surrounding villages, ensuring the fame of the forest. For many years the Amalien Oak became the very symbol of Hasbruch.

For her final years the Queen of the forest was sustained by a single strip of bark just 10cm (4in) across, and on 10th February 1982, the Amalien Oak fell. Her remains lie in a large clearing revealing just how large her canopy was. Unlike her namesake however, the Oak left an heir in the shape of the Friederiken Oak.

Of all the oaks of Haßbrook it seems to me at least that which is dedicated to the Queen of Greece, which is now officially known as "Amalien-oak", is the most powerful and also the most beautiful.
From *Nordwestdeutsche Skizzen* by Johann G Kohl 1864

ABOVE: The Amalien Oak by Ferdinand Lindner 1880
OPPOSITE: The Amalien Oak in all her splendour 1906
BELOW: The Amalien Oak, fallen 2014

Friederiken Oak
Hasbruch Forest

The Friederiken Oak *(Quercus robur)* is the largest, oldest and last of the so called 'thousand year oaks' in Hasbruch Forest. A girth of 7.9m (25.9ft) and its tall stature (ancient oaks generally shed their upper canopies as a survival tactic in old age), would suggest an age nearer to 700 years, but its hollowing, gnarled, burl encrusted trunk firmly places it in the final stage of Dryden's eulogy:

Three centuries he grows ; and three he stays
Supreme in state ; and in three more decays.

The tree was named by Augustus, Grand Duke of Oldenburg (1783-1853), after his second daughter Frederica, who was born in 1820, the year her mother Princess Adelheid died. In 1855 Frederica married Maximilian Emanuel von Washington, a distant relative of George Washington, the first President of the United States, but later renounced courtly life and chose to live out her days in Styria, south east Austria, until her death in 1891.

The House of Oldenburg is one of Europe's most influential Royal Houses, and despite its northern German origins, has branches connected to Denmark, Russia, Norway, Greece, Sweden and the current Queen of England Elizabeth II.

In 1967 one of the Oak's secondary branches fell during a storm, and remains where it dropped beside the tree, providing habitat for myriad forest creatures, plants, fungi and other life-forms. The encroachment of young tree growth around the oak encourages further retrenchment as the lower leaves and branches struggle for light. The process of 'haloing' – the cutting back of younger trees which impede light – would give the Friederiken Oak a greater chance of attaining its bestowed millennial status – the last of its kind.

ABOVE: Friederiken Oak 1901
OPPOSITE: Friederiken Oak 2014

The Ivenack Oak Tiergarten, Ivenack

At Ivenack near Stavenhagen in the former East Germany, stands a remnant Oak wood pasture, celebrated for housing the largest Oak tree *(Quercus robur)* in Europe.

The area was grazed by free-roaming livestock, allowing individual trees to grow large, since the end of the first millennium by the Slavic Wilzen tribe. The practice, known as Hudewald, continued in the 1200s with the Cistercian Monks of Ivenack Monastery until the reformation in 1555 when the 'Oaks of Ivenack' passed into the hands of the ducal authority. German tradition holds that the 'best ham comes from under the Oaks', alluding to the feeding of pigs on fallen acorns each autumn.

Turned into a deer park in 1709, the Hudewald continued to be worked until the economic crisis of 1929, when the introduced fallow deer were removed. It was left to grow wild until 1972 when the deer park was re-established, since which time it has been much restored.

Legend tells how seven Ivenack nuns broke their vows by leaving the convent to dance half-naked through the woods, whereupon they were transformed into Oak trees for their sins. After 1,000 years, each nun will be released from their statuesque existence in turn, one every century, as the ancient Oaks naturally die.

The largest Oak in the Tiergarten measures 11.2m (37ft) in circumference and stands around 31m (102ft) tall. Known as the Ivenack Oak, it is Europe's largest Oak tree by volume, containing close to 140m³ of timber, it is a giant of its kind, and Germany's most famous 'thousand year Oak'. The Ivenack Oak's age is estimated at between 750 and 1,200 years old, with most experts assuming an age of around 850 years old. A century ago, eleven ancient Oaks stood in the Tiergarten, but now only six remain, so perhaps the first of the nuns has been released from her thousand year penance.

When with tender Silvery light
Luna peeps the clouds between,
And 'spite of dark disastrous night
The radiant sun is also seen
When the wavelets murmuring flow
When oak and ivy clinging grow
Then, O then, in that witching hour
Let us meet in my lady's bow'r.

From *An Old Story of My Farming Days*
by Fritz Reuter 1878

ABOVE: The Ivenack Oak 1916
OPPOSITE: The Ivenack Oak 2012

Ick far a Eikbom,
de steiht to de Lake
de Nurdsturm de chest in sin Knäst;
proudly stretched hei de mighty Kron
in de Hoh,
so is dat all Dusend Johr wäst.
Fritz Reuter 1810-1874

Dab Jan Bazynskiego
Kadyny

Travelling east from the city of Gdansk across northern Poland you quickly become aware of the flat, agricultural landscape, interspersed with rows of ancient pollarded Willow trees – still worked – and mistletoe-clad Poplars at the roadside.

That is until you near the eastern border, where the monotony is broken by Beech woodland set in an undulating landscape. At Kadyny, just 20 miles (32km) from the Russian border, an ancient, hollow Oak *(Quercus robur)* – Dab Jan Bazynskiego (Jan Bazynsky's Oak) – cuts an impressive figure at the roadside.

At 10.03m (33ft), it is the third largest girthed Oak in Poland, and one of its oldest. It stands on the edge of Kadyny Forest Nature Reserve, a remnant Oak and Beech wood pasture, now dominated by young Beech trees to the detriment of the declining Oaks. In 1880, the tree measured 8.64 metres (28.3 ft), had a door installed and a guard assigned to protect it. A row of Veteran Oaks stand in the shadow of Dab Jan Bazynskiego, the undisputed elder of the clan, thought to be upwards of 700 years old.

The Oak is named after Jan Bazynski (1394-1459), a German-born Knight who, after initially serving the Teutonic Crusaders who ruled the area around Kadyny, became dissatisfied with their order and led an uprising against them that resulted in control returning to Prussia. Bazynski was made Governor of the neighbouring town of Elblag by King Casimir IV of Poland, and from his castle stronghold at Malbork, protected the region against continued attacks from the Teutonic Knights, surviving an assassination attempt in the process. He later died at the castle, and was buried at Elblag.

The tree that stood in Bazynski's manor during his lifetime, and may have been known to him, survives, and looks set to continue for generations yet.

ABOVE: Dab Jan Bazynskiego c1940
OPPOSITE: Dab Jan Bazynskiego 2014

Dab Jan Kazimierz Bakowo

At the village of Bakowo in north-central Poland, around 62 miles (100km) south of Gdansk, stands a largely twentieth century mansion in the grounds of a former medieval palace. Fields to the east host five ancient Oaks *(Quercus robur)*, remnants of a bygone age, reminders of Royal Europe's medieval wood pasture.

Four of the Oaks – all hollow, each with the hollows opening on their northern sides – measure around 7m (23ft) in girth. But one of the trees dwarfs the others in both size and years.

At 10m (32.8ft) in circumference, totally hollow, mossed with age, supporting lichen and invertebrates, at around 700 years Dab Jan Kazimierz is one the oldest, largest and most striking trees of its kind in the country.

It was named after Poland's last monarch from the house of Vasa – John II Casimir – an unpopular Catholic King who abdicated in 1668 to pursue a monastic life in France. He is remembered as having preferred diplomacy to warfare, a virtue that did not stop him launching successful military campaigns against both Russia and Sweden, and lobbying for support against invading Ottomans, an action he would not live to see fulfilled.

Previously, the land housed Wankau monastery containing separate quarters for both Monks and Nuns, where the mixing of the sexes was strictly prohibited. Legend tells how a young sister was imprisoned in the monastery cellars for breaking the rule. However, this did not deter the monks who embarked on digging a secret tunnel towards the nuns. The tunnel collapsed, engulfing the nunnery, the void becoming the lake visible today.

Ghosts of the nuns are said to haunt the site, their screams and moans audible from beneath the ground.

Casimir relegated warfare to its proper place as the instrument of politics, and preferred the councilchamber to the battle-field.
From *Encyclopedia Britannica* 1911

ABOVE: Dab Jan Kazimierz by Jan Matejko 1838-1893
BELOW AND OPPOSITE: Dab Jan Kazimierz 2014

The Linner Linde, a friend of the people.

ABOVE: The Linn lime c1910

BELOW: One of the huge branches - itself the size of a mature Lime tree

OPPOSITE: The Linn Lime 2012

The Linn Lime

Linn

The Lime or Linden tree *(Tilia x europaea)* at Linn in northern Switzerland is thought to be some 800 years old. Standing at the northern edge of the village with a colossal hollow trunk measuring 10.75m (35.2ft) in girth, supporting a fine burgeoning canopy, Switzerland's oldest and widest broadleaf tree has a tragic story to tell.

In the 1660s, the village was hit by the area's worst ever outbreak of plague. Two thirds of the local residents perished, including the undertaker employed to cart the bodies to a distant cemetery. So instead, the dead are said to have been laid to rest by a lone survivor who buried them in a common grave, at the foot of the great Lime tree.

It would seem that the spot was not simply chosen as a means to an end. The Lime tree was consecrated to the pagan goddess Freya by Teutonic peoples – the mother goddess – associated with love, fertility and death, and thought to ward off evil spirits. Indeed, the Linn Lime has been a local meeting place for centuries, upholding ancient European tradition where the Lime is central to the community – a place for celebrations and dancing and a venue for the local court of law.

The tree itself is no stranger to trauma. Over the years several fires have been lit within its hollow bole, all of which were thankfully extinguished, and in 1990 the Lime survived an attempted poisoning. A large opening on the southern face of the trunk is now protected by wire mesh, and the huge branches – each the size of a mature Lime tree – are roped together in an effort to prolong the longevity of the tree.

The name of the village probably derives from Linde, German for the genus of the tree, and an emblem of the Lime adorns the local post office (above).

A sign informs that should you be feeling the strain, a few minutes beneath the tree will calm and revive you. It certainly worked for me after a four hour drive from Lake Geneva. Drinking a tea brewed from the fragrant Lime flowers has long been held to have the same effect.

86

The Morat Lime
Fribourg

On 22nd June 1476, the Swiss Confederate army fought a decisive battle against the forces of Charles I, Duke of Burgundy at Morat (or Murten), near Berne. Charles had been expanding his empire from the north, but the Swiss had beaten the Burgundian in a battle at Grandson in March of that year. Allowing him to escape, Charles regrouped, eager to redress the embarrassment of his earlier defeat, and on 10th June he laid siege to the city of Morat.

The Swiss had other ideas, and totally crushed the unprepared Burgundians twelve days later, suffering the loss of only six to seven hundred troops compared to deaths of around ten thousand on the Burgundian side. Charles escaped once again, but the battle effectively spelled the end of the Burgundian dynasty and Charles was killed the following year at Nancy whilst fighting the French.

The story goes that a Swiss messenger ran from the scene carrying a lime branch plucked from

the battlefield, waving it as a victory sign. He ran 17km (10.5 miles) to Fribourg, where he collapsed, exhausted. The branch took root on the spot and became known as the Morat Lime.

In truth the tree was probably much older than this and survived until 1983 when a drunk driver crashed into it. On removal, a cutting was taken and replanted in front of the Hotel de Ville (town hall), beside a fountain dedicated to St George slaying the dragon.

The young Lime tree *(Tilia cordata)* is doing well, its trunk having already grown to 1.6m in circumference (5.25ft) and continues the original gene pool. The famous runner is also remembered in the annual Murten to Fribourg race, where some 8,000 participants from all corners of the globe follow his footsteps on the first Sunday in October.

But ere these matchless heights I dare to scan,
There is a spot should not be pass'd in vain, –
Morat! the proud, the patriot field! where man
May gaze on ghastly trophies of the slain

From *Childe Harold's Pilgrimage* by Lord Byron 1812-1818

OPPOSITE: The Morat Lime 1887

LEFT: The Morat Lime and Market Place 1892

ABOVE: The descendent Morat Lime 2012. The position of the original tree is marked by the red monument to the right

The Legend of William Tell

The national hero of Switzerland, William Tell, was born in the village of Burglen in the centre of the country.

Whilst visiting Altdorf with his son Walter in 1308, he publicly refused to bow in front of a pole that had been erected in the town square for the purpose by the Austrian lord, Hermann Gessler.

Infuriated by his insolence, and aware of Tell's prowess with a crossbow, Gessler condemned the pair to death unless the hero could shoot an apple from the head of his son.

Walter was put against a Lime tree, an apple placed upon his head. William told him not to be afraid, took aim and split the apple in two from fifty paces with a perfect shot, leaving the boy unharmed.

Noticing that Tell had pulled two bolts while loading his bow, Gessler asked him why? Tell replied that the second bolt was for the lord, should his son have come to harm. In a rage, Gessler had William Tell arrested and taken by boat across Lake Lucerne to prison. But a furious storm broke out, and the fugitive escaped, jumping onto rocks when the boat came close to shore. Making his way to Küssnacht, Tell found Gessler, and killed him with the second bolt from his bow.

These revolutionary acts are said to have sparked a rebellion in which he took part, and acted as a catalyst for the foundation of the Swiss Confederation.

GESS. (points to the boy.) Bind him directly to that lime tree.
WALTER. Bind me! No, I will not be bound.
I will stand as still as any lamb.
From *William Tell: a play* by Friedrich Schiller 1829

ABOVE: William Tell shoots the apple from his son's head beneath the lime tree, from Rossini's Opera cards by Liebig 1938

Le Marronnier Officiel

Geneva

Since 1818, the Sautier of Geneva has recorded the first leaf of a certain Horse Chestnut tree that stands on the Promenade de la Treille at the edge of the old town, each and every year. The occasion is known as l'éclosion (the budding), and officially marks the first day of spring in the city.

The tradition was started in a non-official capacity by a local patrician Marc-Louis Rigaud-Martin in 1808 to satisfy his own curiosity. But since 1818, the date has been recorded on parchment, and is held in the neighbouring Hotel de Ville.

Being one of the first trees to bud in spring, it is hardly surprising that a Horse Chestnut (*Aesculus Hippocastanum L.*) was chosen for the purpose. Previously, two other trees grew in the same location, the first from 1818 to 1905, the second from 1906 to 1928. The current Marronnier Officiel (official Chestnut) was planted in 1929, and has grown to a healthy 2.4m (7.8ft) in girth, despite leaning at an angle of some 30 degrees or more, requiring support to its primary branch from a metal A-frame.

Annually, l'éclosion is celebrated on the third Saturday of March in the shade of the tree as 'the Fête de la Première Feuille', or the Celebration of the First Leaf, but it seems that the budding approaches earlier each year.

In the nineteenth century a March/April date could be expected, but throughout the twentieth century the buds have arrived successively sooner – in February and March between 1970 and 1989, in January and February from 1990 to the present day, with a record-breaking bud appearing on 29 December 2002, meaning that two official entries appeared on the record for that year, but none for 2003. A barometer for global warming? Perhaps, but 2012 saw the budding return to a more conventional March date.

In curves the yellowing river ran,
And drooping chestnut-buds began
To spread into the perfect fan,
Above the teeming ground.

From *Sir Lancelot and Queen Guinevere* by Alfred Lord Tennyson (1809-1892)

ABOVE: Le Marronnier Officiel 2012

Giant Ficus   Cadiz

In 1903 a hospital was built near the seafront in Cadiz, sponsored by one of the city's greatest benefactors; José Moreno de Mora.

Spain may be better known for its Cork Oaks, Pine and pollarded Black Poplar trees, but at the Plaza del Hospital de Mora, stand two famous Banyan trees *(Ficus Magnonioide)*. The trees had been brought to Spain from India by a missionary nun who had been stationed there. Returning to Spain by ship, she became ill and died a patient in the Mora hospital. As a mark of respect, the two trees were planted in front of the hospital entrance. As with many Fig trees, the species has a symbiotic relationship with the fig wasp that pollinates the tree – the only way it can reproduce. In the right conditions the tree can reach great proportions.

After just over a century the Banyans in Cadiz have reached a massive 9.8m (32ft) and 10.5m (34.4ft) in circumference, and dominate the square. The branches have wandered to such an extent that concrete pillars were raised to support them. At night, the trees are lit to spectacular effect and attract many visitors amidst the chaos and pollution of busy traffic.

In 1990, the hospital was closed and has since been home to the Faculty of Economics and Business of the University of Cadiz.

Tales of hauntings in the building abound, especially around the library (the old mortuary). One such ghost story describes the terrifying sight of a nun wearing a habit full of blood. Surely not the missionary from India returned to Cadiz in sinister guise...

There is in Cadiz quite a passion for flowers, which is gratified, in some degree, by the inhabitants of the city buying all those brought from the gardens of Puerta del Santa Maria.
From *An Encyclopedia of Gardening* by John C Loudon 1828

ABOVE: The young Ficus trees at Plaza del Hospital Moro c1915
BELOW: The Giant Ficus trees at Plaza del Hospital Moro 2011

Millennial Olives Ibiza

The Phoenicians arrived in Ibiza in 654 BC during the westward expansion of their empire across the Mediterranean. They brought with them their beloved cultivated Olive trees *(Olea europea)*, which are thought to have originated in their Lebanese homeland, and while not native to the western Mediterranean, are today naturalised and recognised as synonymous with the region's culture and define its boundaries. Spain is currently the world's largest olive oil producer.

The Phoenicians named the white island Ibosim after Bes, God of music and dance – two arts that over 2,500 years later, the island is still famed for.

2,000 year old amphorae containing olive-oil recovered from the sea-bed near Ibiza town – the old Phoenician port – were remarkably well preserved. The Greeks knew it as Pityûssai; Pine Island, after the Aleppo Pine *(Pinus halepensis)* that once covered the island, and can still be found foresting the interior, especially in the more mountainous, rural areas.

On the lower slopes amongst the fruit and almond trees stand numerous Olive groves. Some millennial Olive trees still remain, some thought to be 2,000 years old, reminders of their ancient origins, survivors of the many cultures that have passed through the island since they were planted. Phoenicians, Egyptians, Greeks, Carthaginians, Vandals, Moors, Catalonians, hippies and more recently 24-hour-party-people have all plied their trade here, and dined on the olive-rich Mediterranean cuisine said to be part of one the healthiest diets in Europe.

ABOVE LEFT: Millennial Olive tree south of Sierra de la Mala Costa 2008
ABOVE RIGHT: Tree of Life by Kimberley Thomas 2008
LEFT: 3m girthed millennial Olive tree, Sant Joan de Labritja 2008

93

Tasso's Oak Rome

Torquato Tasso was a sixteenth century poet, highly regarded in his field and widely read throughout Europe from his lifetime into the nineteenth century.

Born in Sorrento in 1544, he completed his most famous work aged 31 – La Gerusalemme Liberata (Jerusalem Delivered), a fictional retelling of the crusades and the taking of the holy land.

Dogged by mental illness and depression – probably schizophrenia – Tasso struggled to match his epic poem in later life. He spent a large part of it living in the castle of Ferrara in northern Italy at the court of his patron Alfonso II, but was committed to St Anna asylum by the Duke for seven years when his mental health deteriorated.

He wandered between Florence, Rome and Naples, finally returning to Rome to accept a Laurel crown from the Pope in recognition of his life's work as 'King of Poets' – the Poet Laureate.

Legend has Tasso waiting for his award on Janiculum Hill beneath a large Oak tree. The highest point in Rome, it affords commanding views across the city and the Vatican. But Tasso was to die at the age of only fifty one, before his honour could be bestowed, and was buried at Sant'Onofrio church further down the hill.

Flanked on each side by four surviving Sessile Oaks (*Quercus petraea*), Tasso's Oak still stands on the hillside – long dead – its decaying form supported by girders, iron hoops and a commemorative brick wall, each individual brick etched over decades with graffiti.

In stark contrast, nineteenth century paintings by Salomon Corrodi and Maxim Nikiphorovich portray the Oak in proud health. Surviving a lightning strike in 1842, the photo from 1910 (right) shows the tree in good leaf, but it died soon afterwards, and following an arson attack in 2013 the tree and its environs benefitted from a restoration program in 2015.

Love is when he gives you a piece of your soul, that you never knew was missing.
Torquato Tasso 1544-1595

RIGHT: Torquato Tasso
BELOW: Tasso's Oak c1910

The shooter grew,
the broad-leaved sycamore,
The barren plantain,
and the walnut sound,
The myrrh, that her foul sin
doth still deplore,
The alder owner of all waterish
ground,
Sweet juniper, whose shadow
hurteth sore,
Proud cedar, oak, the king of
forests crowned;
Thus fell the trees, with noise
the deserts roar;
The beasts, their caves, the
birds, their nests forlore.

From *Gerusalemme Liberata*
(*"Jerusalem Delivered"*) by
Torquato Tasso 1581 Translated
by Edward Fairfax 1600

LEFT: Tasso´s Oak 2015
BELOW: Graffiti beneath Tasso´s
Oak 2015

95

Cork Oak   Gallura, Sardinia

The Cork Oak (*Quercus suber*) is different to most Oaks in that it is an evergreen, keeping its holly-like leaves year round. The tree possesses a unique ability to regrow its thick, spongy bark after removal – a process which has facilitated its removal for centuries, making it a precious resource. It has been suggested that this regeneration developed as an evolutionary response to forest fires, enabling the tree to redevelop quickly compared to other trees and suffer less damage.

Native to the north and west Mediterranean in an arc spanning from Morocco to Croatia, Cork Oak forests are harvested every nine to twelve years, allowing the bark time to regenerate without causing harm to the tree. Spain and Portugal are the foremost providers, with Portugal supplying fifty percent of the world market. With a life span of between 150 and 250 years, each tree can be harvested safely a dozen times and produce around 4,000 corks.

Cork has been utilised for over two millennia as a bottle stopper, swimming float and shoe-sole, and is popular in flooring and furniture production, historically sustaining a renewable and environmentally sound method of timber production.

But with the increasing use of screw top and plastic bottle stoppers, the industry and in turn the managed Cork Oak forests, face a real threat of abandonment and clearance. An age-old family livelihood passed from generation to generation is in danger, as well as the diverse plant and wildlife that has developed in the Cork Oak forests, with endangered species such as the Iberian lynx and Bonnelli's eagle under serious threat.

Add to that the fact that a harvested Cork Oak stores up to five times more carbon than an unharvested tree, and the importance of their survival and protection seems beyond dispute.

This part of the forest consists of an unbroken mass of primitive cork trees of great size. The rugged bark, the strangely-angular growth of the limbs, hung with grey lichens in fantastic combs, and the thick olive-green foliage almost excluding the light of heaven, with the roar of the wind through the trees.

From *Rambles in the Islands of Corsica and Sardinia* by Thomas Forester 1858.

LEFT: Cork Oak bark stripping, 1885
OPPOSITE: Harvested Cork Oak above the Forest of Gallura, Sardinia 2014

Italian Cork Oak production is firmly centred in Sardinia in the Gallura region around Calangianus in the north of the island. Supplying around 85% of Italy's demands, its primary use is as bottle stopper, but the cork is also used for insulation, flooring, decoration and all manner of kitchen utensils including traditional plates and spoons.

The Romans were the first to harvest the bark in quantities to cork their wine, and also to make their sandals, so it could be said that Rome marched on Sardinian cork. The island became a Roman province in 227 BC, but not without strong resistance from the native and warrior-like Nuraghi people, who continued to be a major thorn in the side of the Romans for over a century, running campaigns from some 7,000 'Nuraghes' – stone built defensive towers that also acted as dwellings – many of which remain in remarkably good condition.

There is great skill involved in removing the cork with a traditional cork axe – cut too deep and the tree will die – and the bark is often removed in just two pieces – one either side of the trunk. It is left to season in the fields for a year before being boiled and then pressed flat, removing the natural curvature of the trunk-shaped pieces. The cork is then graded depending on imperfections, the best quality being reserved to cork the very best wines.

Some Cork Oak trees live for 300 years, such as the great 3m (9.8ft) girthed specimen shown opposite, standing in pasture woodland near Sant Antonio de Gallura. Sardi – the island's indigenous long haired sheep – live in harmony with the trees, grazing in non-intensive flocks amongst the Olive and Cork Oak groves as they have done for centuries. But Sardinia's cork forests have declined by around 30% over the last half century due partly to agricultural expansion and fire but more recently, due to the use of screw-top or plastic bottle stops that are displacing cork, causing abandonment of the Cork Oak forests. Pasture woodland does well as long as it still provides an income, but as the income declines, so does the habitat. The challenge is to uphold the balance for the future. A simple way of aiding the cause is to buy wine with cork stoppers.

ABOVE: Cork seasoning at Calangianus 2014

ABOVE LEFT: Sardi grazing amongst the Cork Oak and Olive groves 2014

OPPOSITE: A veteran 3m girthed Cork Oak (without bark) at Luras 2014. An elder statesman of the Gallura Cork Oak forests, this tree will have been harvested many times throughout its lifetime

Il Patriarca   Santo Baltolu, Luras

... and you would never believe that at night the trees walk or become dreams.
Do you think that in a tree there is a violin of love.
Think a tree sings and laughs.
Do you think a tree in a crevice then becomes alive...

From *L'anima innamorata (The Soul in Love)* by Alda Merini 2000

Beside the Cork Oaks, Olive trees grow in abundance in Gallura. They share the same fortune in that they are both 'working' trees. They have lived, benefited from, and provided for the local people for millennia, which is why they survive today. Like cork, olive oil is extracted on an industrial scale, and Sardinia is famed for the high quality of its extra virgin oil.

In Santo Baltolu, about 9 miles (14km) north of the small town of Luras, stand three venerable Olive trees on a hillside above Lago Liscia – a man-made lake created in 1964 to provide water for the north east of the island. The largest of the trio, Il Patriarca – The Patriarch – has a hollow, wizened trunk measuring 11.6m (38ft) in circumference and covers an area of 600m^2 (1,968ft^2). It is unusual in that it is an ancient Wild Olive (*Olea europea)* of which there are many in the area. These three trees are wild in the extreme, their small inedible fruits supported by flailing branches stretching out, unhindered by the traditional pruning of their cultivated cousins.

Using dendrochronology – the study of tree rings – in direct comparison with another ancient local Wild Olive tree sacrificed for the process, it has been calculated that Il Patriarca may have stood for 4,000 years, making it Italy's oldest tree. If true, this is interesting in that it predates the arrival of the Phoenicians who are generally thought to have introduced the Olive from the eastern Mediterranean around 1,000 BC as they made their first incursions on the island, providing strong evidence that Wild Olive trees were already growing in Sardinia a thousand years earlier, commensurate with Sardinia's Nuraghic warrior elite.

OPPOSITE AND OVERLEAF: Il Patriarcha, Luras 2014

Olivastro de Millenaro

Santo Baltolu, Luras

Beside Il Patriarca, in the same grove, stand two more ancient wild Olive trees, or 'Olivastri Millenari' as they are collectively known. In 1991 the trio were awarded 'Natural Monument' status by the Ministry of the Environment.

The nearest is around 500 years old and bows in an arc towards its elder sibling. The third tree stands at 8.2m (26.9ft) around its girth, and is thought to be 2,500 years old. The striking difference with the two younger trees is that they are not roped off for protection as is the case with Il Patriarca. Walking beneath their branches presents an almost subterranean environment, their drooping limbs creating a dark and cavernous space, heavy with the weight of history, allowing close observation of the gnarled and twisted trunks. Nooks and crannies, hollows and crevices, bark encrusted faces hiding in the shadows – great templates for *Ents* if ever there were.

Although left in a fairly natural state, an entry fee is charged for upkeep of the trees, which does at least provide them with some form of protection. Besides, Sardinia is rightly proud of its elder sylvan statesmen and time-honoured olive heritage. I was told by several Sardinian natives that their olive oil is the 'best in the world', and I must admit that after tasting it, I found it hard to disagree.

ABOVE: 500 year old Olivastro de Millenaro, Luras 2014
LEFT: 2,500 year old Olivastro de Millenaro, Luras 2014

105

Madonie Natural Park

In central-northern Sicily stands the Madonie mountain range, which boasts the highest peaks in Sicily after Mount Etna, with Pizzo Carbonara the highest at 1,979m (6,493ft).

The mountains are ringed by fifteen alpine towns and villages, dating back to medieval times and beyond, and reflecting the rich history of Sicily through its subsequent Greek, Roman, Arab, Norman and Aragonese settlements, strong evidence of which remains in the styles of architecture, art, food and folklore. Villages regularly remain cloaked in thick, misty cloud throughout the day.

The high altitude and micro climate has ensured the area – which covers only 2% of the island – hosts 50% of Sicily's native flora, and all of its mammals including wildcat, wild boar, porcupine, fallow deer, hare, fox and hedgehog. Sometimes referred to as a botanical crossroads, sitting as it does between the continents of Europe, Asia and North Africa, the Madonie is rich in flora from all these areas, and boasts many rare endemic species of its own.

One such species, the Sicilian or Madonie Fir (*Abies nebrodensis)*, is so rare that it has been added to the IUCN Red List of Threatened Species. Only 29 trees remain in the wild, and each subject has been meticulously measured, numbered and catalogued. No 17, the largest of the firs, can be found at Vallone Madonna degli Angeli – Madonna of the Angels Valley – near the town of Polizzi Generosa. Thought to be between 150-200 years old with a girth of 1.85m (6ft), it is also likely to be the oldest growing naturally, but a larger specimen at 2.4m (7.8ft) in circumference stands in the garden of Castello Casale in Polizzi Generosa.

A living fossil, the species disappeared from the rest of the world following the end of the last ice age some 10,000 years ago. They once covered the Madonie mountains, but extensive logging caused major decline, and by 1900 the species was thought to be extinct. The current survivors were not discovered until 1957, since which time efforts have been made to ensure their survival and re-planting on the Madonie.

The beauty of the leafy fronds
The river's sad lament
An aria, the echo that responds
They all breathe sentiment.

Giovanni Meli (1740-1815)
English translation by Arthur & Alice Dieli.

ABOVE: Madonie Fir at Vallone Madonna degli Angeli

On the higher slopes of the Madonie, large groves of Olive trees still grow in abundance, with many ancient trees surviving in areas such as Scillato. The crop, along with sun dried tomatoes, oranges and lemons, provides a mainstay for the many Agritouristo centres in the area – working farms that double as guesthouses – and serve their own fresh produce as part of the bargain.

Forests of Beech *(Fagus sylvatica)* are widespread in the mountains, the furthest south the species are found naturally in Europe, coexisting with the Mediterranean evergreen Holm Oak *(Quercus ilex)*.

At Piano Pomo amongst one such wood nestles a grove of 317 pollarded Holly trees *(Ilex aquifolium)*. Growing to a height of 15m (49ft) with girths measuring up to 8.1m (26.5ft), they are thought to be some of the oldest of their kind in Europe, with individuals reaching 350 years old.

In 1989 40,000ha (98,842ac) of the area was protected as Madonie Regional Natural Park (Parco Naturale Regionale delle Madonie).

Where prickly pears hedge the woods of Avellani and olive trees twist amid chestnut and orange trees and African agaves happily accompany north oak-trees.
From *L'Ora* by Giussepe Antonio Borgese 1905

ABOVE: Olive press at Scillato
BELOW: Ancient Olive trees at Scillato

Castagno dei Cento Cavalli

Sant' Alfio

On the eastern slopes of mount Etna in the village of Sant' Alfio stands probably the largest and oldest Sweet Chestnut tree (*Castanea satia*) in the world – Castagno dei Cento Cavalli.

Translated as 'Tree of One Hundred Horses', it is named after Giovanna, Queen of Aragon, who sheltered beneath the great canopy during a thunderstorm with her retinue of 100 mounted knights in the 15th century, at a time when the Aragonese kingdom stretched from Catalonia to Sicily. Local tradition strongly supports the story, and a square in the village is named after the Queen.

Thought to be around 3,000 years old, the trunk measured a colossal 57.9m (190ft) in circumference in 1780. A hut was erected within the cavity in the early 17th century to store the vast crop of chestnuts – a valuable winter food source. By 1871 much of the tree had decayed, leaving four giant stems which people assumed were separate trees. During this period a track ran between its principal remains, wide enough for a carriage to pass through, causing further damage to the tree over the years.

Villagers believe that Sant' Alfio and the tree are protected from the active volcano by the three saints that the village was named after. In 1929 a lava flow came close, but parted and stopped at the head of the village, near a statue of the saints, still clearly visible today.

The tree was victim to disease carried on ammunition by troops from the Far East during World War II, and suffered from fire in the early 1990s when travellers lit a barbecue inside one of the hollow stems, which remains blackened from the blaze.

At present only three trunks remain, one of those half-fallen and propped by supports made from its own fallen branches. But on approach the tree certainly appears to be one, and recent DNA testing confirmed that all stems share the same root system, proving that the great Chestnut is in fact one huge organism.

Suffering from a rotting disease which experts are managing to hold at bay, Castagno dei Cento Cavalli still produces a plentiful supply of chestnuts which still taste good after 3,000 years of fruiting. The tree is lucky to have a new guardian in the form of Alfio – a local volunteer who proudly holds the key to the secure metal fence built in the 1990s to protect it. In 2008, UNESCO declared the tree a Monument to Peace.

A chestnut tree was so large that its branches formed an umbrella under which refuge was sought from the rain from thunder bolts and flashes of lightning by Queen Giuvanna with a hundred knights, when on her way to Mt Etna was taken by surprise by a fierce storm. From then on so was it named this tree nestled in a valley and its courses the great chestnut tree of one hundred horses.

Giuseppe Borrello (1820–1894)

ABOVE: The Hundred Horse Chestnut 1837
BELOW & OPPOSITE: The Hundred Horse Chestnut 2012

Il Castagno della Nave

Sant' Alfio

Meanwhile the said Musumeci, despite the injunction ... cut with so much boldness said four chestnut trees that lie on the ground, and cry at the destruction of these respected monuments because of a hand so barbarous.

Landolina denounces Musumeci to the Minister of State Soratti, February 1812.

Just along the road from Castagno dei Cento Cavalli stands another monumental Sweet Chestnut tree *(Castanea satia)* Il Castagno della Nave or The Ship Chestnut, named after its immense bole which with a little imagination resembles the hull of a ship.

Lying on private land, but clearly visible from the road, the tree has a girth of 23m (75.5ft) at its base, its four principal branches measuring between 6.4m (20.9ft) and 10m (32.8ft) at 1.3m (4.2ft) from the ground, each the size of a large tree themselves. At an estimated 1,800 years old, The Ship Chestnut has a way to go before it takes the mantle from its distinguished neighbour, but ranks as senior to the oldest of its kind in Britain – The Tortworth Chestnut – by a respectable 300 years or more.

Local tradition remembers seven monumental Chestnut trees known as the Seven Brothers in the vicinity, of which this famous pair are the sole survivors. By 1745, measures were taken to ensure their protection by decree of the rectors of the diocese, but in 1812, despite an injunction made to the contrary, one Antonino Musumeci from Mascali cut four of the six down for charcoal burning.

From that point on, the trees have been held as venerable relics of the community. It is a mark of the fertility of Etna's rich, volcanic soil, standing amongst the lemon, Etna Apple trees and Vine groves, that these outstanding Chestnuts have achieved such longevity.

ABOVE: Il Castagno della Nave by Jules Gourdault from Opera di appartenenza 1877
BELOW: Il Castagno della Nave 2012

The Millennium Olive

Sant' Anastasia

Sicily may well be famed for its lemon groves, but Olive trees have thrived on the island at least since the arrival of the Greeks over 2,500 years ago. At that time, Greek colonies were expanding from the Aegean, bringing their customs and precious Olive trees with them. Southern Italy and Sicily became known as 'Magna Graecia' – Greater Greece, and were important strategic outposts which helped to feed the growing population.

To this day, ancient Olive trees are often referred to as Saracen Olives in Sicily, a nod to a century of Arab rule there from around 945 AD. The best Olives are said to grow on Sicily's east coast, where they thrive in the rich, fertile volcanic soils around Etna, where many of the Saracen trees survive.

At Sant' Anastasia, 13km (8 miles) west of Catania, stands one of the oldest (*Olea europea*). Thought to be around 1,200 years old, hollow, gnarled and twisted, with a girth of 8.5m (27.8ft), the Olive tree sits in an ancient grove on a raised bank on private land. Still producing olives, the tree is in good company amongst several venerable siblings, and can be found, fittingly, at the end of Via dell' Ulivo Millenario – Millennium Olive Road.

September brings acorn and olives.

Sicilian proverb.

ABOVE: The Millennium Olive 2012
LEFT: Ancient Olive, Sicily c1920

Körner's Oak

Castle Park, Dalovice, West Bohemia

Archaeology has revealed that there was Neolithic settlement at Dalovice, predating the arrival of the Slavic people who came to populate the country. The castle on the high ground (actually more of a chateau than a castle proper), was completed in 1875 and replaced three former castles, each of which had burnt down, the earliest of them dating to the twelfth century.

The castle park hosts one of the Czech Republic's oldest Oaks (*Quercus robur*), a great hollow, maiden tree measuring 8.87m (29ft) around its waist, standing 18m (59ft) tall. Estimates of its age range from 500-1,000 years, but it fits well with a c1501 planting when the castle was rebuilt.

The tree was named after Theodore Körner, a German writer and soldier, who stayed at the castle in 1811 whilst taking spa treatment at nearby Karlovy Vary, and was sufficiently moved to sit beneath the Oak and compose a poem; 'Die Eichen' during his stay.

In April 1813, Körner returned to Dalovice, this time to convalesce from a severe head wound administered by the sword of a French General during the Napoleonic wars, during a supposed amnesty. Körner spent a fortnight at Dalovice recovering, before shortly returning to the war of liberation against Napoleon. In August of that year however, Körner was hit by gunshot in the forest of Rosenow during a skirmish and fatally wounded, aged 22. He was buried beneath the shade of an Oak tree in the village of Wöbbelin.

In 1914, Baroness Mathilde Riedl von Riedenstein, the then owner of the estate, commissioned local sculptor Ludwig Tischler to produce a statue of Theodore Körner which was erected facing the great Oak.

Nine great Oaks once stood in the park, by the early nineteenth century only five, a century later just three, and by the beginning of the twentieth century only Körner's Oak remained, a remnant of medieval wood pasture, now protected for as long as it will stand.

For know, this oak o'ershadows holy ground :
A valiant band hath chosen me to guard
This grave, and keep it for as brave a heart
As ever beat within the breast of youth.

From *Life of Körner* by Christian Körner (Theodore's father) 1827

Fair image of old German loyalty,
As in better days it has been known,
When, with glad devotion fired, the free,
Dying, laid their country's cornerstone –
Why should I renew the pang? Ah me!
'Tis a pang each bosom feels its own!
Mightiest of the mighty, German land,
Thou art in the dust –
thy old oaks stand!

From *Die Eichen* by Theodore Körner
1811

ABOVE: Körner's statue 2015
OPPOSITE TOP: Körner's Oak 1902
OPPOSITE BOTTOM: Körner's Oak 2015
RIGHT: Körner's Oak 2015

The Petrohrad Oak
Petrohrad, West Bohemia

Following Charles IV's 'Golden Bull' decree in 1356 – which effectively proclaimed the Czech Republic's independence from the Holy Roman Empire – in 1360 Czech nobleman Peter of Janovice built a Gothic castle in rural lands 80km (50 miles) west of Prague. Named 'Peter's Castle' after him (and hence where the village takes its name), Peter created a Bohemian stronghold.

The grounds were laid out in the traditional north European style to wood pasture. By the fifteenth century the castle was desolate. A lookout tower was erected and remains amongst the castle ruins.

However, good evidence of Petrohrad's medieval origins survives to the south west of the castle. At 9.18m (30ft) in circumference and around 22m (72ft) tall, one of the Czech Republic's largest, oldest Oak trees *(Quercus robur)* stands in a small clearing by the roadside. Hollow, yet robust and vigorous in growth, the deeply furrowed, mossy bark cloaks a 750 year old tree, most likely planted shortly after the castle was built.

By that time, Bohemia's dominant faith was Christianity, but the pagan cult of Svantovit, followed by the Slavs until 1168 when the Christian Danish King Valdemar violently destroyed their shrine at Arkona, sprang to mind on my visit. Alfons Mucha's 'The Celebration of Svantovit' (1912), one of 20 giant canvases painted by the artist for his Slav Epic, was hanging in the Fair Trade Hall in Prague. Depicting a pagan festival, and the Slavic people's subjugation by Germanic tribes, Svantovit holds his sacred sword aloft to defend the Slavs, spouting prophecies from the crown of a great Oak.

ABOVE AND BELOW: The Petrohrad Oak c1945, 2015

Karlovo Námestí Plane

Prague, Bohemia

Slavic settlements have existed in the foothills around Prague since the 6th century, and moved to the hills for protection preceding the founding of the castle around 880.

The city grew across the River Vltava, forming the old town. Petrin Hill to the south of the castle gives an impression of how the area may have looked before development, rich with Oak, Beech, Hornbeam and Chestnut trees.

In the fourteenth century Charles IV set about creating the 'new town', expanding the city considerably. The central square, opened in 1348 and named after the king (Karlovo Námestí), was at the time the largest in Europe, and hosted the cattle market.

It was turned into a public park in the mid-nineteenth century and laid out to planting. A large London Plane tree (*Platanus x acerifolia*), hollow, twisted and gnarled, standing 17m (55.7ft) high with a base girth of 7.95m (26ft) dominates the treescape. Its lowest branch, almost at ground level, extends several metres before rising vertically, braced by a metal support.

The London Plane is a seventeenth century hybrid of the Oriental and American Plane trees, but the jury is still out as to whether it was first grown in Spain or London (as its name suggests). The species copes well with city life, its flaking bark and shiny leaves deflecting pollution, so it is widely planted in cities throughout the northern hemisphere.

The tree sits in sight of the new town hall, site of Prague's first defenestration in 1419. A large crowd of Hussites, led by Jan Zelivsky, who blamed the church for social problems, marched on the town hall demanding release of their imprisoned comrades. When refused, a stone was hurled at the Hussites, inciting them to storm the building and throw seven council members from the tower windows onto the pikes of the mob below.

For we are like tree trunks in the snow. In appearance they lie smoothly and a little push should be enough to set them rolling. No, it can't be done, for they are firmly wedded to the ground. But see, even that is only appearance.
Die Bäume by Franz Kafka 1913.

BELOW: Karlovo Námestí Plane, Town Hall tower visible backround right 2015

115

The Árpád Oak Hedérvar

At over 800 years old, the Árpád Oak *(Quercus robur)* is thought to be the oldest tree in Hungary. With a girth of 7.22m (23.6ft), it is also quite possibly the widest, but certainly not the tallest. As is natural for Oaks in the latter stages of life, the trunk is completely hollow – you can walk right through – and the crown has been lost, along with several major branches. In fact, only one fruitful branch remains, but when I visited in late April the tree was in full leaf and looked the picture of health. It is still producing a good crop of acorns, evident from the previous autumn's yield which littered the ground. The one large remaining branch creaks ominously in the gentle breeze above.

Located in the churchyard of Hedérvar village in the north west of Hungary, just 5km (3 miles) from the Slovakian border, the tree acquired its name from Árpád – leader of the Magyars who migrated from the Southern Ukraine in the late ninth century. By 900 they had conquered large parts of eastern and western Hungary which they adopted as their homeland.

Legend has Árpád tying his horse to the great Oak whilst journeying from one side of his kingdom to the other, marks on the trunk are said to have been left when he did this. Historically, the tree would have to be at least 1,100 years old for the story to hold any water, but there is a chance that the Árpád Oak is older than its estimated age. Specimens in England and Northern Europe have proved to possess that kind of longevity.

Árpád's great-great-grandson, Stephen, is generally regarded as having united Hungary as a nation, replacing the tribal structure with a system of counties headed by Counts. He was canonised in 1083 and his withered hand, The Holy Right, is kept as a relic in St Stephen's Basilica in Budapest. The Árpád dynasty survived until 1301.

Today, the Oak has protected status, and has been supported by a large wooden A-frame since 2007. It hosts colonies of wasps, ants, beetles and a myriad of invertebrates. It stands amongst the graves of bygone Counts of Hedérvar and a former Hungarian Prime Minister, Khuen Héderváry Károly (1888-1960).

ABOVE: King Arpad leads the eight Magyar chiefs that swore allegiance to him as he holds the vezerekkel – a blood oath signed by all in their own blood. To renege on the oath was punishable by death

BELOW AND OPPOSITE: The Árpád Oak 2012

The Köszeg Chestnut
Köszeg

Matthias has died, justice is gone. Hungarian proverb

Nestled in the King's Valley at the foothills of the Alps, just a mile from the Austrian border, stand the remains of a giant Horse Chestnut tree (*Aesculus hippocastanum*), a native to south east Europe.

First noted by the historian Kalman Chernel in 1864, the tree was donated to the Royal city of Köszeg in 1917 by its then owner Gusztav Czeke. When the photograph was taken in 1930 (opposite) the hollow trunk had grown to a colossal 10.5m (34.5ft) in girth, making it probably the largest tree in Hungary. The Chestnut breathed its last in 1963, never to leaf again, and was finally cut down in a state of near collapse in 1981.

A section of the tree is displayed beneath a custom-built roof, and represents the original size of the bole. I hastily measured it at 9.5m (31ft), so as not to disturb the colony of bees that had taken it as their home. Considering that the bark has long since gone, this confers faith in the earlier measurement.

Tree ring analysis showed 330 remaining annual growth rings. Adding to this an estimated 150 rings for the missing hollow part of the trunk takes the germination of the tree to the 1480s, specifically the period when the Hungarian king Matthius the Just conquered Köszeg back from the grip of the Austrian emperor Friedrich III.

Stands of mature Horse Chestnut trees line the hillside of the King's Valley, which leads to the medieval town of Köszeg less than a mile away.

Köszeg was central to the third wave of Turkish attacks on Hungary in 1532, when Miklós Jurisich held the 14th century castle there for 15 days when besieged by a force of 80,000 men led by Grand Vizier Ibrahim. To commemorate the occasion, since 1777 the church bells in the town have rung at eleven o'clock – the hour when the Turks withdrew their attack.

The remains of the Köszeg Chestnut stand as one of many monuments to Hungary's long and turbulent history. But they also reflect the Hungarian mythological belief that the world was represented by the Tree of Life. The Upper World was found in the foliage where the gods lived, the Middle World around the trunk where humans and mythological creatures dwelled, and the Underworld beside the roots, where the spirits of the evil dead and Ördög, creator of pests resided. Only the shamanistic táltos could move between the three worlds. Upon death, people's souls would find either eternal peace in the Otherworld, or eternal damnation in the Underworld depending on how well they had spent their lives – an early precursor to heaven and hell.

Opposite page: The 800 year old Chestnut at Köszeg c1930
Left: Sectional remains of the old Chestnut 2012

The False Acacia Budapest

The False Acacia or Locust tree *(Robinia pseudoacacia)* is the national tree of Hungary yet it was only introduced to Europe from North America in 1601 by J. Robin, principal gardener to the French royalty. Nowhere else did it grow so well as in Hungary, to the extent that the tree became naturalized, and now accounts for 20% of Hungarian forest cover.

At over 150 years old, the specimen in Széchenyi István Square on the east side of the River Danube is thought to be the oldest tree in Buda, (Pest lying on the west bank of the river), near Chain Bridge that first joined the two parts of the city in name and geography. The gnarled, twisted, leaning trunk reflects its age, and is supported by wooden props. But the tree still flowers with droplets of white in summer, producing pollen that makes the fragrant acacia honey for which Hungary is famous.

The False Acacia 2012

The Michael Jackson Memorial Tree Budapest

As a green poplar leaf in wanton play
Dances for joy at rosy break of day.
Garcilaso de la Vega c1501-1536

There is a handsome Black Poplar tree *(Populus nigra)* a species common to Hungary, growing in central Budapest. It is neither ancient nor giant, but nonetheless deserves a mention for a unique reason.

On his three visits to Budapest, the singer and dancer Michael Jackson stayed in the presidential suite at the Kempinski Hotel. Across the road in Erzsébet square, fans gathered beneath the Black Poplar to catch a glimpse of their idol at his window, and were often rewarded with a wave from the King of Pop.

Following his death in June 2009, Michael's Hungarian fans dedicated the tree in his honour, naming it 'The Michael Jackson Memorial Tree', and to this day hang photos, drawings and posters of his image on the trunk, plant flowers and light candles in his memory on the anniversary of his death.

Each year on Jackson's birthday, 29 August, fans hold a 'flashmob' in the streets of Budapest and perform a re-enactment of a Michael Jackson dance routine.

ABOVE AND LEFT: The Michael Jackson Memorial Tree 2012

121

No silver nor gold, not life itself could replace the reward of thy pure and sublime grace.

From *Dubravka* by Ivan Gundulic 1628

ABOVE: The Giant Planes at Trsteno 1909

OPPOSITE: The largest of the Giant Planes 2011

The Giant Planes Trsteno

In the medieval coastal village of Trsteno, just 19km (12 miles) north of Dubrovnik, stand two of the largest Oriental Planes *(Platanus orientalis)* by volume in Europe. The pair are thought to be survivors of an original five trees brought as gifts by a visiting diplomat from Constantinople. They were planted over 500 years ago around a spring in the market place, where they have provided shade and majestic splendour ever since.

In 1806, Napoleon Bonaparte passed through the square with his invading army on his way to Dubrovnik during the expansion of his empire. A sizeable limb from the largest of the two Planes had fallen and blocked their path. It took Napoleon's army two days to clear the way, during which time the Governors of Dubrovnik negotiated safety for the city, whilst the local priest did the same for the trees.

In the 1960s the largest of the pair escaped calamity when a local man tried to remove a hornets nest located inside its hollow 11.73m (38.5ft) girthed trunk, by fire. The fire brigade saved the day.

During the Yugoslav Wars however, the well-being of Trsteno was more difficult to secure. In October 1991, the Yugoslav People's Army attacked by air and sea, destroying a large part of the arboretum which stands adjacent to the great Planes, in an effort to subjugate local culture.

Forest fire caused further damage to the arboretum in 2000, with 48,562ha (120,000ac) lost to burning, but miraculously the Plane trees survived both of these disasters unscathed.

A car collided with the larger of the trees in the 1990s leaving a scar, but failed to inflict any real damage. Then in 2007 the Plane dropped a large branch, which sadly killed a French tourist. This led to the reduction of the tree crowns and erection of fencing for safety. A principle remaining branch is supported by a concrete column.

When I asked my father to photograph the Planes during an Adriatic cruise, time evaded him and he very nearly missed his boat home, but not before he got his tree.

Plato's Olive Athens

See there the Olive Grove of Academe
Plato's retirement,
where the Attic Bird
Trills her thick warbl'd notes the summer long
From *Paradise Regain'd* by John Milton 1671.

ABOVE: Plato in his academy, by Carl Johan Wahlbom from the Swedish Family Journal (1864-1887).

According to Greek mythology, the origins of the Olive tree lay with Athena, goddess of war and wisdom. Both she and Poseidon, god of the sea, laid claim to being patron of the city of Athens. To settle the dispute, Zeus, king of the gods, declared that they should offer a gift to the citizens of the city, who would choose a winner. At the Acropolis, Poseidon struck the ground with his trident and created a salt water spring, while Athena presented an Olive tree. The tree was deemed more beneficial, able to provide shade, timber, fruit and oil. Athena was declared patron, and the city was forever named after her.

Every year, a Panathenaic festival was held at Athena's temple on the Acropolis to celebrate the birthday of the goddess. Festivities included a parade, animal sacrifice, presentation of a robe to Athena's statue, and prizes of money or olive oil for winners of sporting and musical contests.

About a mile (1.6 km) to the north west of the city stood an ancient grove of Olive trees dedicated to Athena, which was spared out of respect by the invading Spartans around 404 BC, as they also revered the goddess. The site would become the academy founded by Plato, famed philosopher, mathematician and student of Socrates, c387 BC. Teaching continued there until 86 BC, when the Roman general Lucius Cornelius Sulla laid siege to the city of Athens, destroyed the Academy and felled many trees to fuel his war effort.

However, at least one tree survived, or perhaps regrew from its rootstock, and became known as Plato's Olive (*Olea europea).* By modern times the tree had reached epic proportions, the gnarled and hollow trunk sustaining a few surviving branches, but on 7th October 1976 disaster struck in the form of public transport when a bus crashed into the tree, uprooting it. The remains of the bole were taken to the Agricultural University of Athens, where they were preserved and displayed in a glass case. Once more, Plato's Olive is resident at an educational establishment, and the university planted a new Olive tree in its original position.

If Plato's Olive was indeed a survivor of the original sacred grove, beneath whose branches Plato held his classes, Aristoltle being one of his pupils, then the tree could be upwards of 2,500 years old.

*And when timber began to fail, ...
he laid hands upon the sacred groves,
and ravaged the Academy, which
was the most wooded of the city's
suburbs...*

From *The Life of Sulla* by Plutarch 1st
century AD.

LEFT: Plato's Olive c1920

ABOVE: Remains of the trunk of Plato's
Olive at the Agricultural University of
Athens

125

Elia Vouvon
Ano Vouves

Olives have been cultivated on Crete since the third millennium BC, an occupation which formed the basis of Minoan economic dominance in the Mediterranean for 1,000 years. Named after King Minos of Knossos, keeper of the mythological Minotaur, the Minoans are said to have been the first major European civilisation. Surviving records from the period clearly illustrate the importance of olives in their culture and economy.

Following the catastrophic volcanic eruption of Thera, some 100km (63 miles) north of Crete, the more warlike Myceneans from mainland Greece took the opportunity to move in and plant their feet firmly under the table. Interestingly, dendrochronology – the dating and study of annual growth rings in trees – provides a date of around 1628 BC for the explosion. Ancient Bristlecone Pines in California and Bog Oaks studied in Ireland show reduced growth rings in this period, illustrating how far-reaching the devastating effects of the eruption were.

Sometime after the demise of these great civilisations, a cultivated Olive was grafted onto the trunk of a Wild Olive tree in the vicinity of Ano Vouves in western Crete. Some 3,000 years later the tree still stands. Hollow and twisted – a living sculpture – the tree appears to have been spun rather than grown, and on closer inspection a number of faces seem to peer out from the gnarled trunk, embedded in the bark.

When Mr Karapatakis built a house there in 1957, he was advised to remove the tree, but realising the significance of the ancient Olive (*Olea europea Masteoidis)*, he decided against that course of action, and donated it to the municipality who declared it a Monument of Nature by special decree.

In 1994 carbon dating offered an estimated age of over 3,000 years old. Graves in a nearby village dating to 700 BC confirm human activity in the vicinity during that period.

I measured the hollow girth at 7.42m (24.3ft). A superfluous statistic when you consider its great age.

Her mother gave her some smooth olive oil in a golden flask, so she and her attendants could use it when they bathed.
From *The Illiad* by Homer c800BC

ABOVE & OPPOSITE: Elia Vouvon 2012
BELOW: The Olive Tree under a rare snowfall 2004

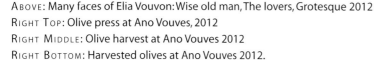

ABOVE: Many faces of Elia Vouvon: Wise old man, The lovers, Grotesque 2012
RIGHT TOP: Olive press at Ano Vouves, 2012
RIGHT MIDDLE: Olive harvest at Ano Vouves 2012
RIGHT BOTTOM: Harvested olives at Ano Vouves 2012.

In ancient times, Greek Olympians were awarded with olive wreaths as marks of distinction. In 2004, the Games of the XXVIII Olympiad were held in Athens, and in commemoration, a branch was cut from the esteemed Olive at Ano Vouves during a special ceremony to make a wreath to crown the winner of that years men's Marathon race.

Each October, a harvest ceremony is held in Ano Vouves where local representatives and dignitaries make speeches declaring the importance and quality of Cretan olives, then take turns collecting olives from the ancient tree – still producing fruit after three millennia. On my visit in 2012, two large baskets were filled with olives, from which oil was pressed to be given as gifts to special guests and visiting luminaries.

Today, 25% of the island of Crete is covered in Olive groves, providing employment for almost the entire agricultural population. No wonder that the Olive tree is held in such high esteem by the locals, not only is the oil Crete's premier export, but Cretans themselves consume more per head than any country in the world.

The Olive tree has symbolised peace, prosperity, wisdom and purity since the earliest times. The Olive at Ano Vouves upholds this tradition on the island of Crete – birthplace of the gods Zeus and Athena – and long may it continue.

The Dromonero Plane

Dromonero

Travelling south from Ano Vouves, ever higher into the mountains amongst circling buzzards and vultures, I spotted a large Oriental Plane tree (*Platanus orientalis*) at the roadside and stopped to investigate. I found myself parked next to an even larger specimen, a giant in fact, and could not believe my luck. A local woman approached and told me enthusiastically that this particular tree was a thousand years old – at the very least.

A girth of 7.9m (25.9ft) may suggest a younger age, but the squat, twisting trunk and hollowing principal branch lend credence to its antiquity. Standing as a focal point in the village of Dromonero, the Plane acts as natural shade from the scorching Cretan sun, offering stunning, elevated views across the western hills of Crete.

Letters will be carved in the bark, so that someone passing by may read in Doric: "Reverence me. I am Helen's tree."
From *The Epithalamium of Helen* by Theocritus 3rd century BC

It is uncertain whether Oriental Planes are native to Greece and her islands, but it is clear that the species was sacred to the ancient Greeks. King Agamemnon made a sacrifice beneath a Plane tree to curry favour with the gods on leaving for Troy, and Helen herself – the face that launched a thousand ships – had a sanctuary in a grove of Plane trees at Sparta. Local place names attest the presence of the tree in Crete such as Platanes and Platanias.

Images of Dadalus and his ill-fated son Icarus spring to mind here – the location is perfect as a launch pad for man's maiden flight, traditionally thought to have taken place on Mount Ida some 100km (62 miles) east as the crow flies.

Did Dadulus construct the first hang glider in his attempt to escape the wrath of King Minos?

The Monumental Olive
Palea Roumata

Continuing south from Dromonero, along winding mountain roads leading through ever-older Olive groves, you find the historic village of Palea Roumata. Sited at the head of the Vavouledo Gorge, a central point between the north and south coasts of Crete, the village hosts an ancient monumental Olive tree. With a trunk measuring 10.5m (34.4 ft) at 0.8m (2.6ft) from the ground, the tree is thought to be as old as the famous tree at Ano Vouves, around 3,000 years, sharing the first appearance of the species *Olea europea Masteoidis* – known locally as 'Tsounati' – on the island of Crete.

Where this tree differs to the one at Ano Vouves however, is that it sits amongst an ancient grove of a dozen or so Olives, aged between 500 and 2,000 years old. Before the advent of the motor car, Palea Roumata must have been fairly innaccessible to the casual traveller, and this partial remoteness, coupled with the shielding effect of the surrounding hills from adverse weather, has helped the historic grove survive the ravages of time. Many trees were lost however in an unusual freezing snowstorm in February 2008.

The village has managed to keep its rural identity and traditional agricultural economy – young, working Olive groves sit comfortably beside their distinguished elders.

During the Ottoman occupation of Crete between 1669 and 1898, rebel Christian villagers hid weapons in a pithos (large pottery storage jar) buried within the cave-like hollow trunk of the monumental Olive at Palea Roumata.

Some two centuries later in 1941, Nazi Germany invaded Crete by air, landing 17,000 paratroopers on the island. The invaders suffered such heavy losses from local resistance armed often only with rocks and farm tools, that Hitler vowed never to repeat the operation. A council was held beside the tree to discuss rebellion, and once more the great trunk became a weapon store.

ABOVE: Plaque at Palea Roumata showing Cretan civilians defending their land from German paratroopers in 1941

BELOW: A young Olive grove nestled beside distinguished elders at Palea Roumata, 2012

OPPOSITE: The Monumental Olive tree 2012

Hippocrates' Plane Kos Town

There was a time in the distant past when the island of Kos was heavily forested. It remains one of the greenest isles of Greece, but successive occupation by Greeks, Egyptians, Romans, Crusaders, Turks, Nazis and Italians took its toll on natural timber resources. It was not until 1947 that Kos regained its Greek status, which explains the strong Greek military presence there today.

One tree survived the invasions and trauma, and is said to have stood in Platanou Square in Kos Town since it was, as legend has it, planted by Hippocrates himself some 2,400 years ago. Named after the famed father of western medicine, Hippocrates' Plane tree is a giant Oriental Plane *(Platanus orientalis)*, supported by a green metal cage which obscures the view of the tree. Without it, the hollowed, decaying trunk would struggle to support its prodigious canopy. Turkish columns that previously held that role mostly collapsed in a devastating earthquake that flattened much of the town in 1933.

The tree is said to have borne witness to Hippocrates teaching his pupils beneath its shade and St Paul preaching the gospel during one of his missions. In those times, before the construction of the Castle of Knights of St John directly to the north of the tree, the elevated plateau of Platanou Square would have offered commanding views across the sea to Turkey. Its darkest hour came in 1821 when 92 Koan citizens were hung from the tree's branches by the ruling Turks for assisting with the fight for Greek independence.

On 5th September each year, local women take an old and a new wreath made from Olive branches, fruit, and leaves from Hippocrates' Plane. They throw the old wreath into the sea, and place the new one at the water's edge to be lapped by 40 waves. On their return home they pass by the tree and touch the trunk to take strength from its longevity, marking the start of their new year.

Medical students from around the world gather at the tree to recite the Hippocratic oath, a pledge to medicine that has been sworn for 2,400 years.

I measured the circumference of the trunk at 6.25m (20.5ft), but judging from archive photographs and the visible earlier footprint of the tree, I estimate that it was previously twice that size.

A remnant of the once larger bole, still in leaf, helps uphold the theory that the tree has grown from a common root system. With hope, when the current tree gives up the ghost, branches at the western end of its walled enclosure will take on the mantle and continue the legend.

I will use treatment to help the sick according to my ability and judgement but never with a view to injury and wrongdoing.
Hippocratic Oath 4.

LEFT: Hippocrates Plane Tree 1910
RIGHT: Hippocrates Plane Tree 2013
OPPOSITE: The gaping hollow trunk of Hippocrates' Plane Tree 2013

Hippocrates is thought to have been born around 460 BC at Kefalos, on the western most peninsula of the island – the opposite end to Kos Town where Hippocrate's Plane tree stands. The second oldest Plane tree on the island grows next to the abandoned Monastery of St John at Agios Ioannis, 7km (4.3 miles) south of Kefalos, has a large trunk and low propped branches, but is not nearly so impressive as Kos' most famous tree.

Travelling east, as Hippocrates would have done on his way to Kos Town, you pass through Plaka, the largest remaining Koan Pine forest, populated today by peacocks and popular as a picnic destination for locals wanting to escape the heat of the Koan sun.

To the west of Kos Town stand the island's most impressive and important archaeological remains in the form of the Asklepion, a sanctuary dedicated to Asklepios – the Greek god of healing. Built amongst a sacred grove of Cypress trees dedicated to Apollo (God of light, father of Asklepios), physicians interpreted the dreams of the sick to diagnose cures for their illnesses and ailments, and sacrifice burnt offerings to the gods.

Natural forces within us are the true healers of disease.
Atrributed to Hippocrates

ABOVE: Statue of Hippocrates, Kos town 2013
BELOW: Sacred Cypress trees surround the Asklepion 2013

Hippocrates worked and studied at the Asklepion, but his great contribution to medicine asserted that illness was caused by natural process, as opposed to a punishment thrown down by the gods. His methods focused on patient care and prognosis, relying on the healing power of nature, administering natural healing from herbs and plants, with rest and immobilisation being a big factor in the healing process. Hippocrates and his school of followers were the first to diagnose many medical conditions.

Hippocrates' fame spread far and wide during his lifetime, and he found himself very much in demand across the ancient world for his healing abilities. The Hippocratic Oath attributed to him is still sworn across the globe, expressing the very essence of ethical medical practice.

In 2006 The Hippocratic Botanical Gardens were opened not far from the Asklepion, where so far 140 of the 250 species of herb and plant thought to have been used by Hippocrates and his followers as natural remedies all those years ago, have been grown.

RIGHT: Pine tree at Plaka 2013

BELOW: Olive grove from the Hippocratic Gardens 2013

El Drago Milenario
Icod de los Vinos

When a Dragon dies, it becomes a Dragon Tree. So holds the legend on the Canary Islands, one of the only places in the world – along with Madeira, Cape Verde, and western Morocco where the tree grows as a native.

The largest and oldest Dragon Tree *(Dracaena draco)*, on the Canary Islands stands in an enclosed garden at the Parque del Drago in the town of Icod de los Vinos, in the north-west of Tenerife. El Drago Milenario is thought not to be so old as its name suggests; 600 years would seem to be nearer the mark, but its colossal size – 10m (32.8ft) in girth and over 20m (65.6ft) tall, has led some to claim it has stood for 1-2,000 years.

Sacred to the original inhabitants of the island – the Guanches – who worshipped at altars inside the hollow cavernous trunks, Dragon Trees were also used to make dug-out boats, tambourines and traditional fighting sticks, and often painted with the red sap of the tree. Known as Dragon's blood, the sap turns red when it comes into contact with air. It was drunk mixed with milk and taken to relieve stomach complaints as well as applied to wounds to aid healing. It continues to be used as a dye, most notably for staining the wood of Stradivarius violins during the 17th and 18th centuries.

The noted German botanist and explorer Alexander von Humboldt visited an even larger Dragon Tree at Franchy Gardens on Tenerife in 1799 en route to south America, and noted that its trunk measured 13.7m (45ft) in circumference. Blown down by a storm in 1867, it leaves El Drago Milenario as the undisputed King of the Dragons. In 1985 its hollow trunk was fitted with a ventilator to minimise fungal growth, and a road that passed by its south side was removed in 1993. The tree now sits in botanic gardens, fenced off from the many visitors that it lures to its den.

ABOVE: Drago, from Northrop's *Earth, Sea and Sky* 1887
OPPOSITE AND BELOW: El Drago Milenario 2013

They built boats from the Drago tree which they dug out whole, put in stone balast and sailed with oars and palm sails around the shores of the island.

Leonardo Torriani 1590

LEFT: Large supported Drago at Icod de los Vinos 2013

ABOVE: Dracaena draco from The Iconic Encyclopedia of Science, Literature and Art 1851

Magnificent as El Drago Milenario may be, Dragon trees of giant proportions are few and far between, which is why Tenerife is so keen to protect its finest example.

Another giant Dragon tree, although not so monstrous as El Drago Milenario, can be found further uphill at Icod de los Vinos. It stands in an open courtyard amongst residential buildings, its hollow trunk is crumbling near the base and liable to collapse, a situation un-hindered by the colony of non-native bees that nest inside. The head of the tree is supported by a metal collar held by chains on three sides. I fear the tree will not get the chance to outlive its distinguished nearby cousin.

In the town of La Laguna in north-east Tenerife stands another outstanding ancient Dragon tree (see photograph right). Growing in the grounds of Santo Domingo Church, previously a convent, it is said to have stood prior to the arrival of the Spanish who conquered the island in 1496, defeating the Guanches in a bloody battle in the Aguere valley where the town was built – the first capital of the island.

The Spanish would not have it all their own way; the conquest followed a year of fierce resistance from Guanche warriors, who inflicted heavy losses on the Spanish, using only sticks and stones in pitched battles against the superior fire-power of the European invaders. Once in control, Spain was quick to assert its dominance over Tenerife's original inhabitants, who knew the island as 'Achinech', and banned them from using their native tongue under pain of death. Thus, the ancient languages and customs of the Guanches are largely lost, but descendants survive to this day.

ABOVE: Drago tree at La Laguna c1905

LEFT: Young Drago tree in the botanic gardens, Icod de los Vinos 2013

139

Laurisilva Forest
Anaga Mountains

The Canary Islands are first mentioned by Homer, who tells of Phoenician travellers visiting around 1,100 BC. The first settlers are thought to have arrived from North Africa, likely from Berber origins, around 500 BC. Greeks, Romans and Vikings all visited, no doubt contributing to the native Guanche gene pool.

In the north of the island where the climate is more temperate than the south, great primeval Laurel forests known as Monteverde (*Lauracae*) grew on the mountain slopes, absorbing cloud moisture blown in on the trade winds from the Atlantic. Water slowly dripped down from the sponge-like lichens hanging from the trees and heather, creating springs and waterways once abundant in the mountains of Tenerife. The Guanches felled parts of the Laurel forests by fire and grazing, driving at least two species to extinction (*Quercus and Carpinus*). Following the conquest, Spanish settlers set about indiscriminately felling them in earnest, clearing land for agriculture, timber and charcoal burning.

When the fountains and waterways dried up in the early sixteenth century – their source denied – the cutting of the forests was prohibited. Much of Tenerife's water is now imported from the Spanish mainland by boat.

Preceding the last ice age around 8,000 years ago, this kind of Laurisilva forest was widespread across southern Europe and North Africa, and had been for at least 3 million years. Encompassing some 15 species of Laurel, today it is found only in Macaronesia – literally 'happy islands' – and part of Morocco, where warm and humid growing conditions suit. Similar forest can be found in America, Madagascar and Australasia.

In Tenerife, the best remnants of the ancient forest survive high in the Anaga mountains above the town of La Laguna, in the north east of the island. Relicts of Paleo-tropical Tethyan flora, the dense canopy provides habitat for birds including the Canary, and some rare species of butterfly. Only an estimated 12% of the original Laurisilva forest remains, but natural regeneration occurs across Macaronesia (except in Gran Canaria where the forest was devastated), as the economy moves from one of agriculture and forestry to tourism.

I have never beheld a prospect more varied, more attractive, more harmonious in the distribution of the masses of verdure and rocks, than the western coast of Teneriffe.
Alexander Von Humboldt 1799

LEFT: Dense Laurel Forest with mosses and ferns 2013
OPPOSITE: Laurel Forest on the Anaga mountains, showing the extent of previous deforestation, looking west across La Laguna towards El Teide 2013

Pino Gordo
Vilaflor

Wherever you go when visiting the island of Tenerife, it is difficult to ignore the towering peak of El Teide, Spain's highest peak at 3,718m (12,198ft) above sea level.

An active volcano which last erupted in 1909, its name derives from the Guanche 'Echeyde' meaning hell. Legend says that the volcano once held Guayota (the devil), imprisoned by the supreme Guanche god Achamán. Eruptions spew forth little bits of hell on earth, fired by Guayota's seething anger.

High on its southern and eastern slopes between one and two thousand metres (3,300-6,500ft) above the sea, stand the remains of a pine forest endemic to the Canary islands. The Canarian Pine *(Pinus canariensis)*, that previously ringed the volcano on all sides was heavily logged following the Spanish conquest. Notable for its long needle-like leaves, which grow up to 30cm (12in) in length, ideal for absorbing moisture from the trade wind clouds, it is also one of the most fire resistant conifers in the world, protected by its thick bark, and capable of growing new shoots from its trunk after fire.

Just north of Vilaflor – Spain's highest municipality at 1,400m (6,500ft) above sea level – stand two giant Canarian Pines which escaped the woodman's axe. The largest of the pair Pino Gordo (The Fat Pine), stands 45m (147.6ft) tall, with a girth of 9.4m (30.8ft). It is the largest of its kind in the world and certainly the largest pine I have ever seen. At up to 1,000 years old, the tree remains in remarkably good health, and receives a constant stream of visitors on their way to the peak of El Teide. Nearby stands a taller, but younger sibling of Pino Gordo known as Pino de las dos Pernadas 57m (187ft) tall, with a girth of 8.34m (27.3ft). Thankfully the remaining Canarian Pine forests are now protected.

ABOVE: Canarian Pine forest with El Teide beyond 1903
OPPOSITE: Pino Gordo 2013
BELOW: Pinos de las dos Pernadas 2013

The Holy Tree

Mataria, Cairo

King Herod was visited by Magi from the East – the three wise men – inquiring as to the whereabouts of the new king of the Jews. Rather than celebrate the news, he sent orders to kill all boys in his kingdom under the age of two years old in order to protect the title for himself.

Mathew's gospel tells of an angel who warned Joseph of the impending doom, urging him to escape from Palestine with his family to Egypt, which he duly did.

According to Coptic Christian tradition, preserved in a manuscript recounting a vision of Pope Theophilus, Patriarch of Alexandria (384-412), after traversing the northern desert, they stopped at Heliopolis, ancient Annu – city of the Egyptian sun god Ra. Their holy presence is said to have shattered the pagan idols, causing the family to flee from angry locals intent on revenge. Sheltering beneath a Sycomore Fig *(Ficus sycomorus)*, they sought refuge from the mob within its hollow trunk, hidden from view by a spider's web, and escaped unharmed.

Sited in the modern day district of Mataria, about 10km (6 miles) north east of Cairo, a descendent of the tree still stands, and is revered as a holy relic and a place of pilgrimage. The current tree is said to have been grown from a cutting in 1672 which in turn was grown from a previous cutting. It is the oldest of its kind in Egypt.

In 1869, the tree was offered as a gift to the Empress Eugenie to take back with her to France at the inauguration of the Suez canal. She declined the offer, wondering instead if she could take the skeleton of the spider that spun its famous web.

Sycomore Figs have been cultivated in Egypt for 5,000 years. The ancient Egyptians named them Nehet, the tree of love, and prized their fruit, shade and timber. Coffins and furniture of the dead made from its hardwood have been found in ancient tombs. The latex-like sap has many medicinal uses, including the treatment of skin disorders.

Today only 300 or so specimens survive in Egypt. The wasp responsible for pollinating its flowers has become extinct, which leaves the tree in real danger of following a similar fate.

And when they were departed, behold, the angel of the Lord appeareth to Joseph in a dream, saying, Arise, and take the young child and his mother, and flee into Egypt, and be thou there until I bring thee word: for Herod will seek the young child to destroy him.

When he arose, he took the young child and his mother by night, and departed into Egypt: And was there until the death of Herod: that it might be fulfilled which was spoken of the Lord by the prophet, saying, Out of Egypt have I called my son.

From *The Gospel According to Matthew* 2:13–15.

LEFT: The Holy Tree 1878   BELOW: The Holy Tree c1920
OPPOSITE: Joseph, Mary and Jesus at the Holy Tree, Chapel of the Virgin c1910

Then Abram removed his tent, and came and dwelt in the plain of Mamre, which is in Hebron, and built there an altar unto the Lord.

Let a little water, I pray you, be fetched, and wash your feet, and rest yourselves under the tree: ... and he stood by them under the tree, and they did eat.

From *Genesis* 13:18, 18:4,8

ABOVE: Abraham's Oak c1905

OPPOSITE: Remains of Abraham's Oak 2010

Abraham's Oak Mamre

At Mamre, just 3km (2 miles) from Hebron, stand the remains of the oldest tree in Israel, a Palestine Oak *(Quercus pseudo-coccifera)* held to be 5,000 years old. The tree's name comes from the belief that it is the spot where Abraham pitched his tent and entertained three angels, who told him that his 90 year old wife Sarah would soon expect a child.

Also known as the Oak of Mamre or the Sibta Oak, it is doubtful whether the tree is quite as old as suggested – Oaks rarely live longer than 1,500 years – but it could well be a descendent of the original sacred tree. Traditionally, Abraham was thought to have lived in the second millennium BC, but recent evidence proposes that he may have lived in the first.

During the reign of the Roman Emperor Hadrian (117-138), it is said that no less than 135,000 Jewish slaves were sold at market in the shade of Abraham's Oak. In the twelfth and thirteenth centuries European crusaders visited the tree where they held the 'Feast of the Trinity' – a celebration of Abraham's legendary meeting with the angels.

The photograph from 1905 shows a huge trunk, dwarfing the Palestinian man standing beside it. The principle branch – struck by lightning and torn off in 1852 – left a stump clearly visible on the left. That branch alone yielded eight camel-loads of timber.

The wood was thought to prevent illness, and successive visits by souvenir hunters have taken their toll. The Oak is now protected by a metal cage, and continued to bloom until 1996 when it died, leaving a twisted, decaying trunk bound in iron and supported by metal and wooden props. But the ageing sentinel has done well to make it this far, surviving Egyptian, Canaanite, Israeli, Assyrian, Babylonian, Persian, Greek, Roman, Byzantine, Arabian, Crusader, Ayyubid, Mameluk, Ottoman and British rule, but sadly not, it appears, that of modern Israel.

The Zacchaeus Tree
Jericho

48km (30 miles) north east of Mamre as the crow flies, but nearer 128km (70 miles) by road, is the site of the reputed, and sometime disputed 'oldest city in the world' – that of ancient Jericho – which could be 10,000 years old. Known as the 'City of Palms', this Jordan Valley oasis is still rich in date palm trees.

According to Luke's Gospel, Jesus passed through here on his way to Jerusalem. Zacchaeus, a local tax collector, being of short stature, climbed into the branches of a Sycomore Fig tree to get a better view amongst the crowd. On seeing him, Jesus invited Zacchaeus to come down from the tree, for he wished to dine at his home. The crowd was shocked that their saviour would mix with such an unpopular person as the tax-man, but Zacchaeus, touched by the love of Jesus, publicly repented his sins and hosted a feast as requested.

A large Sycomore Fig (*Ficus sycomorus*), said to be the very one that Zacchaeus climbed, still stands in the garden of the Holy Land Museum, hollow trunked with a circumference of 7m (23.4ft), and a height of 18m (60ft).

A site of pilgrimage, in the year 2,000 the tree was found to be unhealthy, so the Russian owned cultural centre had the Russian Agricultural Institute remove a colony of termites and dead growth as part of a regeneration programme, which saw the tree fruit once more. After tests the Institute declared it to be 2,000 years old, upholding the belief that it could be the very tree that Zacchaeus climbed.

The Sycomore has a contender nearby at the Greek Orthodox monastery, where the remains of a huge dead Sycomore Fig trunk are preserved in a glass case, and it is believed by some that this is the famed tree. For me the former tree has the edge – not only has it survived two millennia of war and upheaval, but it stands as a beacon of hope and longevity as Palestine struggles to secure its future.

And Jesus entered and passed through Jericho.

And, behold, there was a man named Zacchaeus, which was the chief among the publicans, and he was rich.

And he sought to see Jesus who he was; and could not for the press, because he was little of stature.

And he ran before, and climbed up into a sycomore tree to see him: for he was to pass that way.

And when Jesus came to the place, he looked up, and saw him, and said unto him, Zacchaeus, make haste, and come down; for to day I must abide at thy house.

From *The Gospel According to Luke* 19:1-5

ABOVE: Zacchaeus and the Sycomore tree 1911 postcard
OPPOSITE: Zacchaeus Tree 2013

The Tree of Agony
Garden of Gethsemane, Jerusalem

Following the Last Supper, the Gospels tell how Jesus left the city of Jerusalem and made his way with Peter, James and John to the Garden of Gethsemane on the Mount of Olives. In this favoured spot, Jesus instructed his disciples to watch him while he prayed, and to stay awake so as not to fall into temptation. Twice the followers fall asleep, and twice Jesus wakes them. The third time he leaves them in their slumber and continues his prayer. This was Christ's hour of agony, his '*sweat was as it were great drops of blood*', fully aware that Judas was to betray him with a kiss and present him to the multitude of armed soldiers, priests and servants that would arrest him and condemn him to death by crucifixion.

Gethsemane literally translates from Aramaic as 'oil press', suggesting that Olives have been tended in the area since before the time of Jesus. First mentioned in the fifteenth century, the eight ancient, gnarled and hollow Olive trees (*Olea europaea*) that stand in the garden today may not be the trees that Jesus walked amongst that fateful evening, as Roman soldiers under the command of Titus are said to have cut down every tree in the vicinity during the siege of Jerusalem in AD70. Olives possess the ability to regrow from old root systems, and there is every chance that the Olive trees seen today are descendants of those which clothed the hillside in Biblical times. They have been objects of veneration and pilgrimage ever since.

Suffering in full the guilt of his treacherous actions, Judas Iscariot returned the thirty pieces of silver paid to him by the priests for his betrayal, and hung himself from the branch of a species of tree which still bears his name – the Judas Tree (*Cervis siliquastram*).

As a boy I visited the Garden of Gethsemane during an educational trip in 1978. It was the first time I had seen ancient Olive trees, and the memory stayed with me – especially the part where I spat out the exceedingly bitter olive fruit that had looked so tempting on the tree! How was I to know that Olives need special preparation before they are good to eat?

Then cometh Jesus with them unto a place called Gethsemane, and saith unto the disciples, Sit ye here, while I go and pray yonder.
From *The Gospel According to Matthew* 26:36.

ABOVE: The Garden of Gethsemane from *Narrative of the United States' Expedition to the River Jordan and the Dead Sea* by William Francis Lynch (Commander US Navy) 1894

OPPOSITE: The Tree of Agony c1930

BELOW: The Tree of Agony 2009

The Cedars of God Becharri

The Cedar of Lebanon *(Cedrus lebani)* has been celebrated in Middle Eastern history and folklore since the earliest times. Cedar makes no less than 75 appearances in the bible alone; a symbol of strength, wisdom and longevity, a cultural giant.

Great Cedar forests once spanned the Mount Lebanon range in abundance. The strong timber was durable and easy to work – its fragrant, balsamic, resin resists decay.

The sacred Cedar forests were said to belong to the gods, who lost ownership in a battle for the trees with men intent on harvesting them. The four thousand year old 'Epic of Gilgamesh' makes reference to their felling, a practice most famously remembered in the biblical tale of King Solomon, in order to construct his temple in Jerusalem, Solomon sent *four-score thousand hewers* by arrangement with Hiram the king of Tyre to relieve Lebanon of its sylvan treasure.

Native Phoenicians practically built their empire on the Cedar, constructed their ships and houses from it and traded it with Israel and the ancient Egyptians who valued the resin to mummify their dead. A 2,000 year old 'Jesus boat' recovered from the Sea of Galilee was made of Cedar, as was the golden ship of Egyptian conqueror Sesostris.

Assyrians, Babylonians and Persians all contributed to deforestation, until the second century when Roman Emperor Hadrian declared the forests an imperial domain, which halted their destruction for a while.

Medieval forest clearance for agriculture and 19th century Ottoman activity continued reduction. Queen Victoria commissioned construction of a wall around the remaining grove at Becharri in 1876, to protect it from grazing goats. Felling resumed during World War II when British troops cut timber to lay a railway between Tripoli and Haifa.

A beautiful grove of about 400 trees is all that remains at Becharri, including four ancient specimens, the largest of which measures 14m (46ft) in girth and is thought to be around 2,000 years old. In 1985 the Committee of the Friends of the Cedar Forest initiated a reforestation program and in 1996 Unesco declared the grove a world heritage site.

This old tree is held in almost idolatrous veneration by the villagers living near it. Festivals are held around it, its remaining branches are hung with votive offerings, and what seems to be worship is rendered to it.
Oldest Cedar in Lebanon (opposite) c1915

Top: Transportation of Cedar by ship for Solomon's Temple. From *Biblia* by Keur and Keur 1702
Above: The Cedars of God c1900
Opposite: The Oldest Cedar in Lebanon c1915

The Sisters   Bechealeh

While the Phoenicians may have built their empire on Cedar, they are also thought to have been responsible for introducing the Olive tree on their merchantile travels across the Mediterranean region some 3-3,500 years ago – an action that had far-reaching consequences, shaping the region both culturally and culinarily.

In the small village of Bechealeh, high in the Mount Lebanon range, grow what could be the oldest Olive trees in the world. Equidistant between the Cedars of God at Becchari and the ancient Phoenician port of Byblos, stand a grove of 16 ancient Olive trees *(Olea europaea, Baladi/ Ayrouni: Genotype)* planted in rows and estimated to be around 6,000 years old.

These could be the oldest individual trees on the planet. Gnarled, twisted, perforated and hollow, it is impossible to date the trees by ring-count, but a French archeobotanist visiting the region alledgedly ascertained their age by carbon dating their old-growth wood.

Whatever their age, it is remarkable that the trees have survived so long, on mountainous terrain open to the elements, in an often war-torn area. Their longevity may owe something to local mythology, which claims that they are the very trees seen by Noah after 40 days and 40 nights, when he landed the Ark following the abating of the waters; the same trees from which his scouting dove returned carrying an olive leaf in her beak signifying dry land. Not inconceivable when you consider that the trees grow around 1,300m (4,265ft) above sea level. It is interesting that both the dove and the Olive are international symbols of peace.

Standing on land belonging to the Christian church, whose religion they predate by four millennia, the Sisters Olives still bear fruit. The olives are cold-pressed in small quantities into a high grade olive oil – a practice revived to finance a conservation programme for the trees.

The ministry of tourism and culture has recognised the Sisters as a site of national importance, and the trees have since featured on Lebanese stamps and currency.

And the dove came in to him in the evening; and, lo, in her mouth was an olive leaf pluckt off: so Noah knew that the waters were abated from off the earth.   From *Genesis 8:11*

Top: The Dove returns to Noah, carrying an Olive leaf from *Bible Pictures* by Charles Foster 1897

I will be as the dew unto Israel: he shall grow as the lily, and cast forth his roots as Lebanon. His branches shall spread, and his beauty shall be as the olive tree, and his smell as Lebanon. They that dwell under his shadow shall return; they shall revive as the corn, and grow as the vine: the scent thereof shall be as the wine of Lebanon. From *Hosea 14:5*

ABOVE: The Sisters Olive Trees 2012

The Great Banyan
Botanic Gardens, Kolkata

Native to India and south east Asia, the Banyan tree is thought to have taken its name from Banias, the traders who sold their wares beneath the shade of the tree's branches. A Fig tree, it usually starts life as an ephyphite in the branches of established trees, seeded by birds that have eaten its parent's fruit. As it grows the young tree sends down aerial roots and grows around its host, eventually suffocating it – hence its other name – the Strangler Fig.

The Great Banyan tree *(Ficus benghalensis)* at Acharya Jagadish Chandra Bose Indian Botanic Garden, Howrah, near Kolkata, has grown to support the largest tree canopy in the world covering an area of around 1.5ha (3.7ac).

Estimated to be 250 years old, the 15.7m (51.5ft) girthed trunk was removed in 1925 having hollowed after a fungal attack, leaving a gap in the centre of the tree. The Fig has seemingly failed to notice, as it continues to grow and has already exceeded the 330m (1082ft) boundary road that was laid out to contain it.

Over 3,000 aerial roots have taken to the ground and form a myriad of new trunks which give the tree the air of a small forest as opposed to one individual. It has in effect become its own clonal colony and had already reached an immense size when illustrated in 1886 (below).

The Banyan is the national tree of India, and is referred to locally as the Indian Banyan. It is considered sacred, and often houses a temple, the likeness of a deity, or is simply worshipped itself.

Located on the west bank of the river Hooghly, the botanic gardens were established by Lieutenant Colonel Robert Kyd in 1787, primarily to identify new plants of commercial value for the British East India Company. The gardens were renamed on 25th June 2009 in honour of Jagadish Chandra Bose, the Bengali polymath, and they now host over 12,000 trees and shrubs covering 1400 species and thousands of herbaceous plants.

Opposite: The Great Banyan 1886
This page: The Great Banyan 2011

The Sacred Bohdi Tree

Bodh Gaya, India; Anuradhapura, Sri Lanka

In the fifth century BC, Siddhartha Gautama, son of Suddhoda, chief of the Shakya clan in modern Nepal, was born into a life of privilege, protected from the ills of the world. It was not until his adult life that he ventured from his sheltered environment and witnessed for the first time the sick, the old and the dead.

Siddhartha resolved to give up his life of luxury and set off on a religious quest, such was his concern for the human condition. On his travels he saw much pain and suffering, and eventually came to a place called Bodh Gaya in eastern India. Tradition tells how he sat beneath a Fig tree there, and meditated for 49 days until he found enlightenment, becoming Buddha. For the remainder of his days Siddhartha continued to travel, teaching the Buddhist way towards enlightenment.

The Fig, subsequently known as the Bohdi or Bo tree (*Ficus religiosa*), was revered as sacred – its scientific name reflecting the fact – and in the 3rd century BC was put under special protection by the Emporor Asoka. Asoka's beautiful wife Tissarakkha grew jealous of her husband's sylvan devotion, and poisoned the tree with Mandu thorns, killing it.

Asoka had already sent a cutting of the tree to Devanampyatissa, king of Ceylon (Sri Lanka), who planted it in his capital Anuradhapura in 288 BC. That tree, or at least a descendent of it, still stands – holding the distinction of being the tree with the earliest known planting date.

A cutting was returned to Bodh Gaya, but that was killed by King Puspyamitra during his persecution of Buddhism in the 2nd century BC. Another descendent was destroyed by King Sassanka at the beginning of the 7th century. Finally, a British archaeologist planted another cutting from Anuradhapura in 1881, and that tree remains.

Although the Buddhist culture prohibits use of the tree for firewood, its distinctive heart-shaped leaves provide a remedy to treat many ailments in traditional and Ayurvedic medicine, and are sometimes used as canvases for painting.

Buddha for those seven days, in contemplation lost, his heart at peace, beheld and pondered on the Bodhi tree, with gaze unmoved and never wearying: 'Now resting here, in this condition, I have obtained,' he said, 'my ever-shifting heart's desire, and now at rest I stand, escaped from self. The eyes of Buddha then considered 'all that lives'.

From *Buddhacaritam (Acts of the Buddha)* by Asvaghosha Bodhisattva 2nd century, translated by Samuel Beal 1883

ABOVE: The Bohdi Tree, Bodh Gaya, India 1914
OPPOSITE: The Bohdi Tree, Anuradhapura, Sri Lanka 2013
BELOW: The Bohdi Tree, Bodh Gaya, India 2013

The Wishing Trees

Lam Tsuen

In the village of Lam Tsuen to the north of Hong Kong, stands a temple dedicated to Tin Hau, Chinese goddess of the sea, and two sacred Chinese Banyan trees (*Ficus microcarpa*) known as the Wishing Trees.

Before the land was reclaimed here, the temple stood at the seafront. Built c1770, during the reign of Emperor Qianlong of the Qing dynasty, the tradition of wishing started with an ancient Camphor tree that stood there.

Fisherman returning home wrote wishes on scrolled paper josses, tied them to an orange or kumquat fruit, and threw them into the branches of the tree hoping for good fortune. Known as Bao Die, it was believed that if they stuck, the thrower's wish would come true. The higher the branch where it landed, the more likely it was that the wish would be granted. However, if the Bao Die fell, the wisher was judged to have asked for too much, and their wish would be denied.

The Camphor was lost to fire, thought to have been caused by incense sticks inserted into its hollow trunk, which were traditionally lit before making a wish. So, a large Banyan was chosen instead. It stands at over 200 years old, and on 12th February 2005 dropped a large branch which injured two visitors as it fell. The cause of the incident was thought to have been the sheer weight of Bao Die hanging from the branches, such was the popularity of the wishing tradition, particularly during the Chinese New Year festival. The tree was closed to the public to allow it to time to recover, and a young tree planted to continue the lineage. Wooden racks were installed to allow the hanging of wishes to continue.

Many felt that this was inadequate, so an imitation Banyan tree 15m (49.2ft) tall was erected to fulfil the experience of throwing a wish, complete with oranges made from plastic (Hong Kong's favoured manufacturing resource) that come at a price. So if you visit Lam Tsuen, just be careful what you wish for.

The best time to plant a tree was 20 years ago. The next best time is now. Chinese Proverb

ABOVE: Chinese fruit seller and Banyan, Hong Kong 1910
OPPOSITE: The Imitation Wishing Tree, Chinese New Year 2014
BELOW: Chinese Banyan, Kowloon Park, Hong Kong 2011

The Shiogama Cherry
Kenrokuen Garden, Kanazawa

Leaning, heavily propped and fenced-off for protection, the famous Shiogama Cherry tree was caught on camera in full spring blossom over a century ago (below). The Japanese Cherry tree, *Prunus lannesiana*, producing beautiful flowers 3-4cm (1.2-1.5in) wide, stood in Kenrokuen Garden, known as one of the Three Great Gardens of Japan, (along with Kairaku and Koraku Parks).

Founded in the fifteenth century by the Maeda clan who ruled the surrounding Kaga Domain, Kenrokuen Garden adjoins Kanazawa Castle Park, originally laid out as the official garden of the stronghold for the residing feudal lords.

Inherited from the Shiogama shrine in Miyagi, the Shiogama Cherry tree was planted by the twelfth feudal Lord Maeda Naranaga in the garden of Takezawa villa, which he had built between 1819 and 1822. The tree thrived, growing to a height of 10m (32.8ft) with a girth of 7m (23ft). It withered and finally died in 1957.

The gardens were opened to the public in 1874, and designated a National Site of Special Scenic Beauty in 1985. In 2001 a fifth generation descendent of the Shiogama Cherry tree was planted in its honour.

Each spring, once the Cherry trees are in bloom, people flock to parks, shrines and open spaces to picnic and drink sake beneath the vivid pink canopies. This ancient tradition of Hanami has been celebrated in Japan since the third century, originating at the Imperial Court. The custom spread through the samurai warrior class, and finally to the common people. By the seventeenth century, the Tokugawa shogunate were actively encouraging the practice by planting out areas of Cherry blossom trees.

Known as Sakura in Japan, the fleeting but beautiful blossoms of the tree have come to represent the transient and ephemeral beauty of life itself.

Men must be the colour of cherry blossom, even in death.
From *Hagakure, The Book of the Samurai* by Yamamoto Tsunetomo 1716

LEFT: The famed Shiogama Cherry tree c1910

OPPOSITE: Bee moves in on Cherry blossom, spring 2009

Yamataka Jindaizakura

Jissoji Temple, Hokuto

Japan's obsession and reverence for its flowering Sakura is unparalleled, bestowing a cult-like status on the tree, year after year, generation after generation. Japan's earliest texts, including the eleventh century Tale of Genji – sometimes referred to as the world's first novel – mention the tree often, both literally and poetically, such is the endemic nature of Sakura in Japanese culture. Yet the tree cult is rooted far deeper than a mere millennia, stretching back at least to the prehistoric Yayoi period, and I suspect further still, possibly originating with the Jomon hunter-gatherers who reached Japan via land bridge when it was still joined to the Asian mainland 10,000 years ago.

In April 2015, I caught the tail end of the Cherry blossoms in Kyoto, so travelled North-East to the Southern Alps on the trail of Sakura zensen (Cherry Blossom front) – a favourite Japanese pastime following the cherry blossoms as they follow the climate north. Four train journeys later I arrived at Hinoharu station, an outpost of Hokuto, recently bestowed city status by the amalgamation of several satellite towns and villages. I had planned to hike the 6.5km (4 miles) to Jissoji Buddhist temple, but arriving in the pouring rain with a heavy backpack, I took the station's only taxi to visit what is thought to be the oldest Cherry tree in Japan.

I was met by the sight of the largest girthed Cherry tree in the country, measuring 12.8m (42ft) around its hollow black furrowed trunk, yet standing only a stunted 10.3m (33.8ft) tall, reminiscent of Europe's ancient Oaks, which similarly lose their crowns as a survival strategy in old age. Known as Jindaizakura (divine generations sakura) the Sour Cherry tree (*Prunus cerasus*), is thought to be 2,000 years old, and is said to have been planted by Yamato Takeru, a legendary early 2nd century hero traditionally considered to be Japan's 12th emperor, whose soul turned into a great white bird after death, and flew away.

The tree's surviving branches snake away from the trunk, underpinned by a network of wooden props, the leading branch bandaged at the elbow, supported by a concrete brace.

The decision to follow the Sakura zensen paid dividends – Jindaizakura was in full bloom in the cooler mountain climate, and as I stood in the wind and rain, snow-pink petals falling around me in the mist, the Cherry cult obsession made perfect sense. Delicate, fleeting, colourful blossoms set against an historic, wizened trunk perfectly embodied the fragility and beauty of life against the backdrop of an ancient, honourable culture.

The cherry blossoms had already fallen in the city, as it was late in the Third Month. But in the mountain, the cherry blossoms were at their best, which delighted Genji deeply.
From *The Tale of Genji* by Murasaki Shikibu c1010

LEFT: Yamataka Jindaizakura c1900
OPPOSITE: Yamataka Jindaizakura 2015

It is true, they all thought: the cherry blossoms of spring are loved because they bloom so briefly.
From *The Tale of Genji* by Murasaki Shikibu c1010

ABOVE: The Weeping Night Cherry c1910
OPPOSITE AND BELOW: The Weeping Night Cherry 2015

Weeping Night Cherry
Maruyama Park, Kyoto

Japan's second largest city, Kyoto, was founded as a new capital by Emperor Kammu in 794 as Heian-kyo, partly to satisfy his idealistic vision for Japan's future, and partly to escape influence from the former degenerating capital at Nara.

Laid out in the Chinese grid style across a 5km^2 (3 mile^2) flat valley, surrounded by mountains on three sides, none of the original gardens survive. Maruyama park, the city's oldest, was created in 1886 between the eastern Higashiyama mountain ridge and the seventh century Shinto Yasaka Shrine, where in spring time visitors pass through in droves to celebrate Hanami – as they have since Heian times – beneath the pink blossoms of the park's 680 Cherry Trees.

Central to proceedings, and fenced off in reverence, stands the Weeping Night Cherry *(Prunus Kiku-shidare-zakura)*, lit up after dark to illuminate its arching, cascading branches.

The current tree is a descendent of the original Night Cherry (above left), which stood 12m (13ft) tall with a circumference of 4m (39ft), thought to have been around 200 years old when it died in 1947.

As fortune would have it, Toemon Sano, Sakuramori (Cherry Tree doctor) of Maruyama Park noticed the tree's distress, and propagated three of its seeds, one of which he planted in 1949 to replace its parent. Today the second generation tree is cared for by the current Sakuramori – Toemon's son and namesake – upholding both sylvan and human lineage.

The Karasaki Pine

Karasaki, Lake Biwa

Alongside the Cherry Blossom in Japanese consciousness, another tree that features prominently, although appreciated in different ways, is the Japanese Pine. The Black Pine *(Pinus thunbergii)*, which generally grows near the coast, the White Pine *(Pinus parviflora)* happier further inland, and the Red Pine *(Pinus densiflora)* more variable in habitat, have all been trained and cultured for many centuries.

The evergreen Pine represents longevity and permanence, transcending the seasons, and in gardens, temples and shrines is traditionally pruned annually to exacting standards. Every needle is individually cut to present the appearance of a windswept tree.

The Japanese word for Pine (matsu) also means to wait, so in Heian times, poetically the tree came to represent longing, or waiting, along with all the opportunities inherent for word play, sharing an exact parallel with the English word Pine.

We are, you and me,
Like two pine needles
Which will dry and fall
But never separate.

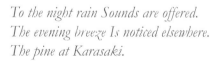

To the night rain Sounds are offered.
The evening breeze Is noticed elsewhere.
The pine at Karasaki.

From *Night Rain at Karasaki* by Konoe Masaie and Konoe Naomichi 1500

ABOVE: Hand-painted Mount Fuji Pine c1910

LEFT: The Karasaki Pine 1904
On the shore of Lake Biwa stands an ancient, multi-layered Black Pine, immortalised in Hiroshige's print *Night Rain in Karasaki* from his *Eight Views of Omi* series. A seed was taken from the tree and planted at Kenrokuen Gardens in Kanazawa by the 13th Lord Nariyasu in the 1830s. It has a 10m (32.8ft) spread like its parent, and is supported by *yukitsuri* – ropes hung in a cone shape to protect the branches from heavy snow

The Buddha Pine   Atami

The night is clear, the moon shines calmly,
the wind in the pines is like a lyre's song.
With no I and no other who hears the sound?
Death Poem by Zoso Royo 1276

At the seaside town of Atami, on the Izu peninsula, a Black Pine *(Pinus thunbergii)*, 4m (13ft) in circumference said to be 800 years old dominates its surroundings. Situated in the grounds of a Buddhist temple, it holds the honour of sharing its domain with a small fragment of bone from Siddhartha Gautama, the Buddha himself, presented to the temple for safekeeping by the Mahabodhi Society in 1966. It remains enshrined unseen within its own locked sanctuary for safe keeping.

Further south, at the other end of the Pine scale in Akao Herb & Rose Garden, stands what is thought to be the world's largest Bonsai tree, a 600 year old Red Pine *(Pinus densiflora)*, 15m (49ft) tall with a 10m (32.8ft) spread.

Down by the beech, there once stood a tree known as Omiya's Pine, named after a scene from Ozaki Koyo's 1897 fictional novel Konjiki Yasha (Devil of Gold). After hearing of her decision to marry a rich man, Omiya's boyfriend Kanichi kicked her as she knelt before him pleading for forgiveness, shouting *"You have been blinded by a diamond!"*, a phrase that subsequently found its way into the popular venacular. By way of consolation, Kanichi went on to live an unhappy and miserly life – some retribution for his violent, callous action.

The original tree fell following a typhoon and was replaced by a new tree in 1966. A section of the original remains under cover.

ABOVE: Buddha Pine, Atami 2015

169

Near to the town, at the temple of "Kinomiya," stands, in a thick grove, an immeasurably ancient camphor tree, the trunk of which is still some thirty feet in circumference.

From *Japan Revisited* by Sir Edwin Arnold 1892

ABOVE: Ookusu c1910

BELOW & OPPOSITE: Ookusu 2015

Ookusu Kinomiya Temple, Atami

Japan's other and more ancient religion is Shinto. In Shinto (literally 'the way of the gods'), spirits or 'kami' were believed to inhabit certain distinctive places in nature, such as waterfalls, rocks and ancient trees. The religion survives and so do some of its natural shrines.

High in the hills above the seaside town of Atami stands one such shrine: a giant Camphor tree *(Cinnamomum camphora)*, 23.9m (78.4ft) in circumference. At an estimated 2,000 years old, the evergreen – known as Ookusu – has its roots in Japan's Yayoi period, at the very beginnings of the Shinto religion, and is the oldest on Honshu Island.

A second, younger tree (at only 1,300 years old) stands close by, hollowed and gnarly like its elder relative. Both trees are delineated with tassled straw ropes known as shime-nawa, a practice denoting sacred status. Medicinal oil and natural painkiller camphor obtained from the tree's bark, further enhance the species' traditional importance.

The pair has survived lightning, earthquakes and tsunami, but before 1859, seven Camphor trees stood at Kinomiya Shrine. A fishing dispute involving the entire village necessitated the raising of funds to cover legal costs, and five of the trees were felled. Legend has it that when the loggers approached Ookusu, a white haired old man appeared and raised his arms which broke the saw in two. The old man disappeared as quickly as he had come, and the villagers took it as an omen from kami inhabiting the tree, whereby Ookusu was spared, and has remained ever since.

Two bows, two claps and another bow are the form of prayer practised at the foot of Ookusu, followed by a lap of the tree to add a year to your life and grant a wish.

A word used to describe an emotional response to transient beauty in nature – awaré – became an essential component of Japanese poetic culture during the Heian period (794-1185). Visiting this tree, I understood it's meaning intensely. It struck me how close in sense and form it is to the English word aware. Could the words share a common, proto-European antecedent?

Jomon Sugi   Mt Miyanoura, Yakushima

A beautiful and stately tree which has no rival except in the Sequoias of California.

From *Forest Flora of Japan* by Charles Sargent 1894

Japan's national tree is the Japanese Cedar *(Cryptomeria japonica)*. Known as Sugi, the tree is endemic to Japan, one of the largest and longest-lived trees in the country.

Long grown for its timber, which is durable and easy to work, it was used to construct many of Japan's historic temples where it was widely planted for aesthetic reasons as well as for working plantations.

Over the centuries, great Sugi forests were lost to logging, but on the small Pacific island of Yakushima, 60km (37 miles) south of Kyushu Island, some spectacular ancient remnants of primeval Sugi forest remain, relics of the Tertiary Period that followed the extinction of the dinosaurs.

High on the north face of Yakushima's highest peak, Mt Miyanoura, at an elevation of 1,300m (4,300ft) almost central to the island, stands Japan's oldest and largest tree – Jomon Sugi – named after Japan's early settlers the Jomon (10,000-300BC).

Old wood taken from the hollow 16.2m (53ft) girthed trunk was carbon dated at 2,170 years old. When compared to other ancient Sugi on the island, (named Yakusugi after reaching the grand old age of 1,000 years), age estimates range between 5-7,200 years old, which if accurate, would make Jomon Sugi the world's oldest tree.

The tree's discovery in 1967 prompted calls for conservation, and in 1993 UNESCO declared Yakushima a World Heritage Site. Tourism now accounts for half of the island's income. In 2005 a strip of bark was stolen from Jomon Sugi. This led to the tree's partition, and it is now only viewable from a platform 15m (50ft) away. Protected, it shares the ancient forest with Japanese Macaque monkeys and Sika Deer.

In 2009, Jomon Sugi was partnered with New Zealand's oldest tree, Tane Mahuta, in a ceremony attended by the mayor of Yakushima who quoted an old Japanese saying; "Do not belittle the Gods of the mountains and the forest, he is worth more than the mountain of money."

ABOVE: Jomon Sugi 2008

Cryptomeria Avenue Nikko

Some 1,500km (932 miles) north west of Yakushima at Nikko on Honshu island, stands one of the longest avenues of trees in the world. 200,000 Japanese cedars (*Cryptomeria japonica*) were planted between 1628 and 1648 by Masatsuna Matsudaira, a Japanese Daimyo (feudal lord), to honour the death of his Shogun, Tokugawa Ieyasu (1543-1616). Ieyasu's son and successor Tokugawa Hidetada had called on the Daimyo for stones and bronze lanterns as tribute to decorate his father's mortuary temple at Nikko Tosho-gu, (a UNESCO World Heritage Site), but according to legend, Masatsuna Matsudaira, pleading poverty, requested to plant an avenue of trees to shade pilgrims from the heat of the sun instead.

Traditional stately processions followed the Nikko Kaido, a route constructed from Edo (modern day Tokyo) the seat of power for the Tokugawa shogunate, to the Nikko Tosho-gu temple complex. Known as 'processions of a thousand warriors' they are still celebrated each spring and autumn.

The Cryptomeria Avenue, comprising three parts, runs for a total length of 35.4km (22 miles). 13,500 trees survive, with an average height of 27m (88.5ft). Some have been replanted over the years, but the larger trees, especially closer to the temple, are likely to be of the original planting, almost 400 years old.

In 2013, an avenue of Dawn Redwood trees (*Metasequoia glyptostroboides*) said to be 47km (29 miles) long was discovered in Jiangsu Province, China. It has yet to be recognised by Guinness World Records, so until then, the Cryptomeria Avenue rules.

ABOVE: Nikko Tosho-gu c1914   RIGHT: Cryptomeria Avenue c1880

When the body of Ieyasu was laid in its last resting-place on the Nikko hills, his successor in the Shogunate called upon the Daimyos of the empire to send each a stone or a bronze lantern to decorate the grounds about the mortuary temples. All complied with the order but one man, who, too poor to send a lantern, offered instead to plant trees beside the road, that visitors to the tomb might be protected from the heat of the sun. The offer was fortunately accepted, and so well was the work done that the poor man's offering surpasses in value a thousand-fold those of all his less fortunate contemporaries.

From *Forest Flora of Japan* by Charles Sargent 1894

The Cheewhat Giant
Pacific Rim National Park, Vancouver Island

Canada's biggest tree can be found in a remote pocket of old growth forest on the south west of Vancouver Island. Known as the Cheewhat Giant due to its location close to Cheewhat Lake, the Western Red Cedar *(Thuja plicata)* lives up to its name with a circumference of 18.3m (60ft) and a height of 55.5m (182ft).

The tree is lucky to have survived at all, having escaped the pervasive attentions of the logging industry. It stands protected in the Pacific Rim National Park, a lush, temperate forest and coastal reserve established in 1971, which covers 511km² (197miles²) of land and sea on Vancouver Island's south west coast. Undiscovered until 1988, The Cheewhat Giant is thought to be 2,000 years old.

The great old growth forests of British Columbia have suffered the effects of clear-cut logging for over a century, a practice that shows no sign of abating. Once felled, so-called sustainable timber plantations are re-planted, littered with old growth stumps. Unfortunately, new growth forest does little to support the biodiversity present in old growth forest, and with a harvest turnaround of 50-60 years, has no chance of developing. Official figures reveal that British Columbia has lost 90% of its original old growth forest to the logging industry.

In stark contrast, the small-scale harvesting practiced by the indigenous peoples is clear. First Nations people revered the Western Red Cedar, and they sought propitiation from the Great Spirit when harvesting it. One legend describes how the Great Spirit provided the tree to be 'useful to all people'.

Organisations such as the Ancient Forest Alliance are working hard to raise awareness of old groves, and promote their future survival through the alternative industry of eco-tourism.

We must protect the forests for our children, grandchildren and children yet to be born. We must protect the forests for those who can't speak for themselves such as the birds, animals, fish and trees.
Qwatsinas (Hereditary Chief Edward Moody) Nuxalk Nation

Above: Removing Bark from a Cedar from *Indian Legends of Vancouver Island* by Alfred Carmichael 1922
Below: The Cheewhat Giant 2009

The Hollow Tree
Stanley Park, Vancouver

When Spanish explorer Captain Jose Maria Narvaez arrived at Stanley Park in 1791, he found a densely forested peninsula, populated with Squamish and Musqueam First Nation people.

The following year, British Captain George Vancouver – after whom both the city that developed south of the peninsula and Vancouver Island were named – arrived to chart the north-western Pacific Coast, and spoke endearingly of the native population.

By 1858 the British had descended in numbers, drawn by the prospect of the Fraser Canyon Gold Rush, but the area was saved from major development when designated a strategic military reserve in the early 1860s.

Native people traditionally harvested timber from the Western Red Cedar *(Thuja plicata)*, from which they hollowed out canoes and carved monumental totem poles, emblematic of their heritage and culture. In 1865 a sawmill was established on the peninsula, and the next twenty years saw no less than six logging companies start work in earnest. In 1888, the peninsula was declared a park, and named after Lord Stanley, Governor General of Canada. The final Squamish house was removed when 'Aunt Sally' Kulkalem, the peninsula's last native resident, died there in 1923.

One of the park's oldest and largest Western Red Cedar trees known as the Hollow Tree or Big Cedar, soon became a popular tourist attraction. A photographer, sensing a business opportunity, set up shop around the tree, and tourists flocked to have their photographs taken around its 19.8m (65ft) girthed heavily burled trunk. In 1910, the photographer successfully campaigned to spare the tree from felling due to a road-widening scheme.

Storms in 1943 and 1962 caused further deforestation, and in 2006, the Hollow Tree's remaining hulk was severely damaged by another storm, though it was already dead by then. Concerned citizens formed the Stanley Park Hollow Tree Conservation Society, and raised enough money by public donation to stabilise the tree and secure its future.

Here we met about fifty Indians, in their canoes, who conducted themselves with the greatest decorum and civility, presenting us with many cooked fish, and undressed, of the sort already mentioned as resembling the smelt.

From Captain George Vancouver's Journal 1792

ABOVE: The Hollow Tree 1926

BELOW: One of nine replica Totem Poles in Stanley Park – BC's most visited tourist attractions. The originals are preserved in the care of museums

Muir Woods   California

300 years ago, California hosted 809,371ha (2,000,000ac) of Redwood forest. The hunger for timber and general perception of trees as a resource led to the felling of huge bands of Redwood forest to the extent that only 60,703ha (150,000ac) – around 7.5% – remain.

One such remnant stands just north of San Francisco, a short trip across the Golden Gate Bridge. It survives thanks to the efforts of William Kent and his wife Elizabeth, who bought the land, and in doing so protected one of the last stands of uncut Coast Redwoods (*Sequoia sempervirens*). They had heard plans were afoot to build a dam, flood the wooded valley and create a reservoir, a project that would have devastated the Redwood forest.

Until then the steep, wooded, hard-to-reach valley had protected the forest from loggers. It provided perfect habitat for Coast Redwoods – the tallest trees in the world – which tower towards the sky absorbing moisture from summer fogs that drift across the coastal hills, essential for their survival.

In 1908 the Kents donated the land to the nation, and it was designated a national monument in honour of John Muir – a Scottish born naturalist who did much to preserve forests and wilderness in the Sierra Nevada – at William's request.

Before the arrival of European immigrants, Native Americans revered and utilised the giant Redwoods, using the bark and timber for shelters, furniture, clothes, baskets and dugout canoes. Some tribes wintered inside the fire cavities of the trees.

Coast Redwood's dense bark – up to 30.5cm (12in) thick – shields it from fire, along with the disease repelling tannic acid that lends the tree its distinctive red colouring. In fact, fire is essential to the trees' survival, enabling seeds to germinate in cleared mineral soils. Fire suppression begun in the

Any fool can destroy trees. They cannot run away; and if they could, they would still be destroyed – chased and hunted down as long as fun or a dollar could be got out of their bark hides, branching horns, or magnificent bole backbones. Few that fell trees plant them; nor would planting avail much towards getting back anything like the noble primeval forests... It took more than three thousand years to make some of the trees in these Western woods – trees that are still standing in perfect strength and beauty, waving and singing in the mighty forests of the Sierra.

From *Our National Parks* by John Muir 1901.

ABOVE: Muir Woods c1910
OPPOSITE: Muir Woods 2014

1880s upset the forests natural cycle, so controlled burning was introduced to redress the balance.

Some of the Coast Redwoods in Muir Woods are over 1,000 years old, 12.8m (42ft) in girth, and 76m (250ft) tall. The tallest Coast Redwood ever recorded stands at 115.55m (379.1ft) tall in Redwood National Park, some 480km (300 miles) to the north of Muir Woods. Discovered in 2006, the giant tree was named Hyperion after the Titan of Greek mythology. Its exact whereabouts are kept secret for its protection.

The Jack London Oak

Oakland, California

In the Bay area city of Oakland stands a lone Coast Live Oak (*Quercus agrifolia*), centrepiece of the grassed Frank Ogawa Plaza beside the towering City Hall.

At 3.8m (12.5ft) in girth, it is neither the largest nor oldest Oak in California, but its story and location bestow a profound significance and marked value on the tree.

Oakland was once the location of the largest Coast Live Oak forest in America. Its acorns were a staple for the native Ohlone people, who ground them to make bread, an important supplement to their thriving fisher, hunter/gatherer lifestyle. The arrival of Spanish missionaries displaced the entire East Bay population by 1795, moving them to the Mission San Francisco, where European diseases against which they had no immunity killed an estimated 61,000 Ohlone people.

In 1852 the city of Oakland was founded, and by the 1870s petitions to fell Oak trees in order to aid development were issued in abundance.

Following the San Francisco earthquake of 1906 which destroyed 80% of the city and killed around 3,000 people, development across the bay in Oakland continued in earnest and large stands of Oak and Redwood from the surrounding hills were felled to rebuild the coastal city. Today, not a single original tree from Oakland's historic Oak forest remains.

On January 16th 1917, a year after the death of America's then most successful writer Jack London, a twenty year old Coast Live Oak from nearby Mosswood Park was planted by Jack's widow Charmian in Frank Ogawa Plaza, at a small ceremony led by Oakland's mayor. Named in Jack's honour, the tree was taken as the city's emblem. Jack had lived and worked in Oakland, formerly as an oyster pirate, latterly writing some of his finest works there. As a young man he orated political speeches by night promoting socialism at that very spot.

The tree remains a poignant reminder of Oakland's lost Oak forest, a mature and vigorous icon, and a touching tribute to the city's most famous literary son.

Ever I planted acorns, making two black oak trees grow where one grew before. And now all is ended. Oh my black oak acorns! My black oak acorns! Who will plant them now?

From *The Acorn-Planter, A California Forest Play*, by Jack London 1916

ABOVE: The Oaks of Oakland 1874
BELOW AND OPPOSITE: The Oakland Oak 2014

178

Oakhurst California

Approximately 600 species of Oak tree can be found across the northern hemisphere; some evergreen, some deciduous, some with lobed leaves and some spiny, but all sharing that common, familiar, cupped seed – the acorn.

North America hosts the highest number of species with around 90 growing in the United States, nineteen of those found in California alone. The reason so many different kinds of native Oak have developed in America is unclear – there are only two kinds of Oak native to Britain, and they cover a large part of northern Europe as well. Looking across the county and its eclectic treescape, from the tallest trees in the world on its western coast (Redwoods), eastwards past the largest trees by volume on the Sierra Nevada (Giant Sequoia), to the oldest trees nestled in the White Mountains (Bristlecone Pines), it may be established that each unique species has adapted to a unique micro-climate, altitude and environment.

The three famous trees mentioned above grow at different elevations across undulating mountain landscapes. The Oaks are found in the foothills and plains below, thriving in the sunlight of the savannah, much as they do in the wood pastures of Europe.

In marked contrast to Oakland's diminished Oak forest, the town of Oakland in the western foothills of the Sierra Nevada still hosts a fair few Oaks. I stopped there on my way to Yosemite, guessing the name Oakhurst may have some sylvan significance, and was pleasantly surprised to find some mature 4.3m (14ft) girthed Valley Oaks *(Quercus lobata)*, growing freely in the town. Surprising, as they stand within earshot of the old town saw-mill previously operated by the California Lumber Company.

Large groves of Valley Oak can still be found in woodland pastures in the surrounding foothills.

ABOVE AND BELOW: Valley Oaks at Oakland 2014
OPPOSITE: Oak pasture to the west of Oakland 2014

Land of the Giants   Calaveras, California

East of the coastal Redwood range across California's central valley rises the Sierra Nevada; (snowy range), 112km (70 miles) wide running 643km (400 miles) north to south, hosting Mount Whitney – the tallest mountain on the United States mainland at 4,421m (14,505ft).

High on its western slopes between 1,370-2,400m (4,500-8000ft) stand remnant groves of the biggest trees in the world. Related to the Coast Redwood, Giant Sequoias (*Sequoia giganteum*), are neither the tallest or the widest, but their bulk qualifies them as the Earth's largest single living trees by volume. Growing to heights of 94.8m (311ft), with circumferences reaching 34.4m (113ft), the oldest recorded Giant Sequoia was found to have an annual ring count of 3,500.

In 1852, Augustus T Dowd was employed as a hunter by the Union Water Company in Calaveras, to provide meat for their workmen. In the spring of that year, having wounded a bear which he then followed in hot pursuit, Dowd was stopped in his tracks when confronted with a Giant Sequoia. Native Americans living in the area for over 3,000 years doubtless knew the groves well, but Dowd was probably the first white man to see the mammoth trees.

On return to camp, Dowd's tale of wondrous giants was met with derision and disbelief, prompting him to show his colleagues proof in person. News of their existence spread quickly, and sightseers flocked to view the spectacle.

The very next year, sensing a business opportunity, the tree first seen by Dowd and subsequently named the Discovery Tree, was felled by gold prospectors. The process took five men twenty two days to complete, after which its bark was re-erected for exhibition in New York, its trunk converted into a bar and bowling alley. However, the exhibition was a spectacular failure.

In 1854, a tree named 'Mother of the Forest' on account of its great size – second only to 'Father of the Forest' which had fallen centuries earlier (opposite) – was relieved of her bark, section by section, destined for display at Crystal Palace in London, via New York. Normally, fire caused by lightning plays a natural part in the life cycle of Giant Sequoias, clearing the ground of competition and triggering the cones to release their seed onto fertile ash. Stripped of its protective bark, in places 60cm (2ft) thick, Mother of the Forest succumbed to fire in 1908. Its burnt out trunk remains, so too the stump of the Discovery Tree, monuments of their former splendour.

The fact that no one in London believed that these trees were real, preferring to imagine the scaffold erected bark as a 'Californian hoax', went some way to support calls at home for the giant forest's protection.

ABOVE: Mother of the Forest 1852

It has been said that trees are imperfect men, and seem to bemoan their imprisonment rooted in the ground. But they never seem so to me. I never saw a discontented tree. They grip the ground as though they liked it, and though fast rooted they travel about as far as we do. They go wandering forth in all directions with every wind, going and coming like ourselves, traveling with us around the sun two million miles a day, and through space heaven knows how fast and far!

Entry from John Muir's Journal 1890

Mariposa Grove
Mariposa Grove, Yosemite

Yosemite's largest and most visited big tree attraction, Mariposa Grove can be found Further south along the Sierra range. Consisting of around 500 mature Giant Sequoias, some reaching 95m (300ft) in height, with girths up to 50m (164ft), the grove survived extensive logging, rampant during the nineteenth century, due in no small measure to the efforts of two early American preservationists.

Galen Clark moved to the mountains for the sake of his health after contracting tuberculosis, and became the first European to explore Mariposa Grove, after hearing of giant trees from a hunter in 1857.

He spent most of the rest of his life there, lived amongst the Giant Sequoia, learning about and then educating others on the wonder of the groves. He wrote a book about the trees and another describing the culture of Native Americans.

The Ahwahneeches lived in the Yosemite Valley for millennia, but were driven out during the Indian war of 1851, and forced to live in Fresno reservation until 1855 when they were allowed to return to their ancestral home, after promising to live in peace. The soldiers who displaced them named the valley Yosemite, mis-interpreting Oohoomate – an Ahwahneeche settlement.

Clark's conservation work was rewarded in 1864, when Abraham Lincoln, breaking from the Civil War, included Mariposa Grove and the Yosemite Valley in the Yosemite Grant Act, protecting the land as California's first National Park. In 1890, the surrounding land was designated Yosemite National Park.

John Muir moved to Yosemite to study its geology and natural history, and in 1903 succeeded in convincing President Theodore Roosevelt of its worth, as they spent the night there camped under the stars. In 1906, Congress combined Yosemite Valley and Mariposa Grove with Yosemite National Park, excluded logging, mining and the grazing of livestock, thereby securing its future.

And I've been to the groves of Sequoia Big Trees,
Where beauty and grandeur combine,
Grand Temples of Nature for worship and ease,
Enchanting, inspiring, sublime!
From *The Big Trees of California* by Galen Clark 1907

ABOVE: The Twins in Mariposa Grove by G Tirrel 1862
BELOW: Galen Clark at the Haverford Tree c1900
OPPOSITE: Big Tree Cabin built around 1860 by Galen Clark, rebuilt in 1930, it now hosts Mariposa Grove Museum 2014

The Grizzly Giant
Mariposa Grove, Yosemite

Originally named the Grizzled Giant after the grizzly bears that once dominated the area during an early survey of Mariposa Grove by Galen Clark in 1859 (the last Yosemite bear was shot around 1895 near Wawona), the Grizzly Giant is today one of the grove's major features attracting up to 10,000 visitors a week during the summer.

Standing 63.7m (209ft) tall, with a circumference at its base measuring 28.2m (92.5ft), it is the largest and probably oldest tree in the grove, and may have reached 84m (275ft) in height before it lost its top.

Blackened and partly hollowed by centuries of sporadic lightning and fire, and leaning at an acute angle, the Grizzly Giant is thought to be around 1,800 years old, falling some way short of Galen Clark's original estimate of 6,000 years, yet still impressive when you consider that the tree is in the prime of life – the 25th largest Giant Sequoia.

The Grizzly Giant is the acknowledged patriarch of the Mariposa Grove of Sequoias... It has a unique individuality of majestic grandeur all its own.
From *The Big Trees of California* by Galen Clark 1907

LEFT: Visitors and Cavalry Rangers at The Grizzly Giant 1903

ABOVE AND OPPOSITE: The Grizzly Giant 2014

One mighty tree that had fallen by fire and burned out, into which we walked for a long distance, we found to be the abode of the grizzly; there he had made his nest, and it excited the nerves to enter so dark an adobe.

From *Scenes of Wonder and Curiosity in California* by James M Hutchings 1862

Wawona Tunnel Tree

Mariposa Grove, Yosemite

Leading uphill from the Grizzly Giant, the winding, forest track eventually leads to the Wawona Tree, once the oldest and most famous tree in Mariposa Grove.

Named after the Native American word for big tree, the Wawona Tunnel Tree stood 69m (227ft) tall with a circumference at base measuring 27m (90ft).

In 1881, sensing a business opportunity, the Yosemite Stage and Turnpike Company paid two labourers – the Scribner brothers – $75 to cut a tunnel through the fire-scarred trunk. At 2.1m (7ft) wide, 2.7m (9ft) high and 7.9m (26ft) long at the base, the tunnel was large enough to allow a horse and carriage to pass through, and became a major tourist attraction.

Over time, visitor laden carriages intent on a good photo opportunity were replaced by convoys of cars and charabancs until 1969, when, weakened by the unnatural chasm cut through its base, the Giant Sequoia toppled over under the weight of a heavy snow storm.

Now known as the Fallen Wawona Tunnel Tree, it remains where it fell, a reminder of its former celebrity status. At an estimated 2,100 years old, the tree may have seen its life cut short by a thousand years. But the high tannin content present in Giant Sequoias – a substance that helps protect the trees from fungal infections, insect attack and fire, responsible for their characteristic red colour – could preserve the giant in its fallen state for another millennia.

Further back down the hill, close to the Grizzly Giant, the California Tunnel Tree, similarly cut in 1895, still stands.

One of those, which measured one hundred feet in circumference, was of exceeding gigantic proportions, and towered up three hundred feet; yet a portion of its top... had been swept off by storms. While we were measuring this tree, a large eagle came and perched upon it, emblematical of the grandeur of this forest as well as that of our country.

From *Scenes of Wonder and Curiosity in California* by James M Hutchings 1862

ABOVE: The Wawona Tunnel Tree 1900

OPPOSITE: The Fallen Wawona Tunnel Tree, 2014

Kings Canyon and Sequoia National Park
California

The name, Sequoia, is the name of a remarkable man, a Cherokee born in Georgia about 1770.

From *The New Book of Trees* by Marcus Woodward c1920

South of Yosemite encompassing the very heart of the Sierra Nevada, sit two National Parks – Kings Canyon and Sequoia. Jointly managed, famed for their great rivers, canyons and mountain wilderness, the parks host the largest Giant Sequoia trees in the world.

The Monaches traditionally lived in King's Canyon, but many of the tribe died tragically in 1862, stricken by smallpox introduced by Europeans, against which they had no natural immunity.

Living on acorns as a staple harvested from Oaks in the foothills, Native Americans built winter shelters using bark of the Incense Cedar, and crafted their bows from Mountain Cedar. In summer, tribes sometimes moved to higher ground, the domain of the Giant Sequoias, from their settlements in the foothills. To them, the trees were sacred, guarded by their sacred deity the owl.

From the nineteenth century, loggers and trappers, followed by hordes of gold prospectors laid waste to large tracts of forest. Ranchers grazed their flocks among the trees suppressing any chance of regrowth. Despite Giant Sequoia timber being brittle, around a third of the old groves were felled in the region.

Due to pressure from conservationists Sequoia and Grant National Parks were created in 1890, followed by Kings Canyon in 1940. These acts would not save the largest stand of Giant Sequoias at Converse Basin, which today resembles a tree mausoleum; a Sequoia graveyard littered with the stumps of the fallen.

RIGHT: Giant Sequoia, Lost Grove, Sequoia National Park 2014

OPPOSITE: Batchelor and the Three Graces Yosemite National Park 2014

The General Grant Tree
Grant Grove, Kings Canyon National Park

A relatively small but important grove of Giant Sequoias spans the north western edge of Sequoia National Park.

Amongst the grove stands The General Grant Tree, named after Ulysses S Grant, President Lincoln's general responsible for leading the Union Army to victory over the Confederates in the American Civil War. He later became the eighteenth President of the United States (1869-1877).

Standing 81.5m (267.4ft) tall, with a girth of 32.8m (107.6ft) at the ground, The General Grant Tree is the second largest Giant Sequoia in the world (when measured by trunk volume).

When Hale Tharp settled at Three Rivers to ranch cattle in 1846, he found the area inhabited by Native Americans, with whom he lived peacefully, Within twenty years, following a large influx of gold prospectors and loggers bringing measles, scarlet fever and smallpox with them, all the native tribes in the area had been displaced.

The General Grant Tree and Grant Grove were the main reasons behind the establishment of Grant Grove and Sequoia National Parks by US Congress in 1890. Grant Grove was eventually incorporated into Kings Canyon National Park in 1940 for its protection.

Proclaimed the Nation's Christmas Tree by President Calvin Coolidge in 1926 after much competition, in 1956 the General Grant Tree was dedicated a national monument by President Dwight Eisenhower to those Americans that had died in war. It remains the only national monument of its kind.

A short distance south of this forest lies a beautiful grove, now mostly included in the General Grant National Park. I found many shake-makers at work in it, access to these magnificent woods having been made easy by the old mill wagon road. The Park is only two miles square, and the largest of its many fine trees is the General Grant, so named before the date of my first visit, twenty-eight years ago, and said to be the largest tree in the world.

From *Our National Parks* by John Muir 1901

TOP LEFT: Ulysses S Grant c1855
ABOVE: The General Grant Tree 1905
OPPOSITE: The General Grant Tree 2014

The General Sherman Tree

Sequoia National Park, California

In 1879, a Giant Sequoia was discovered in Sequoia National Park, and dedicated to General Sherman, who served under General Grant and helped secure Union victory over the Confederates in the US Civil War.

When Grant became President in 1869, Sherman took command of the US Army throughout the Indian wars.

At around 2,000 years old, the General Sherman tree stands 83.8m (274.9ft) tall, with a girth of 24.1m (79ft). Near the ground it measures a colossal 31.3m (102.6ft) in circumference.

It is neither the tallest nor the widest Giant Sequoia, but its total volume calculated at 1,486.9m³ (52,500ft³) makes it the largest single-stemmed tree in the world.

It is perhaps ironic that the tree should have acquired such a namesake – had the Sequoia been in the General's path on his '*march to the sea*', it may well have suffered at the hands of his scorched earth policy of 'total war at all costs'.

Tucked away in the Sierra, despite hollowing from fire, the tree stands defiantly. A branch that fell in 1985 was itself larger than any US tree east of the Sierra.

Archaeological records suggest that Giant Sequoias were present across much of the northern hemisphere in the Miocene period before the ice ages and the ascent of modern humans. A changing climate reduced their native habitat to Oregon and California.

Following their European 'discovery' in 1850, planting of the trees became fashionable, especially on English country estates where many still thrive – returned to their former domain after a five million year absence.

ABOVE LEFT: The General Sherman Tree 1908
ABOVE: The General Sherman Tree 2014

The whole horizon was lurid with the bonfires of rail-ties, and groups of men all night were carrying the heated rails to the nearest trees, and bending them around the trunks. From *Memoirs of General William T Sherman* 1889

The President Sequoia National Park

I grew up on a housing estate near an avenue of Giant Sequoias in the leafy home county of Surrey in England. The trees were planted around 1865 for Augustus Mongredien, the then owner of Heatherside House and Nursery, only thirteen years after the European discovery of the tree 8,000km (5,000 miles) away in California.

Over 200 of those trees survive today, growing up to 7.5m (24.6ft) in girth and 27m (88.5ft) tall, running a distance of one mile through a twentieth century housing estate, deemed too grand to destroy during the development, unlike the forgotten, buried nursery.

As a child I remember punching the soft, red bark with my friends. No damage occurred to either my knuckles or the trees, such was the bark's sponge-like, cushioning effect. To me they stood like mighty giants, stately sentinels; immortal.

My youthful experience with Giant Sequoias may have eventually lead me to visit California some 30 years or more later to visit the trees in their natural environment. But it did little to prepare me for what I would see in the Sequoia groves of the Sierra mountains. Compared to their American cousins, the avenue of trees at Heatherside were mere youngsters, striplings, babes in the wood.

Leading on from the General Sherman tree the 'Congress Trail' winds for two miles through the Giant Forest among named, ancient, sylvan giants in the company of Marmots, Chikarees, Mule Deer and Black Bears.

RIGHT: The President – at 3,200 years the oldest, and third largest living Giant Sequoia by volume measuring 28.4m (93ft) around its base, standing 75.3m (247ft) tall. It was named after President Warren G Harding in 1923, Congress Trail 2014

OPPOSITE: The author debating with The Senate, Congress Trail 2014

Ancient Bristlecone Pine Forest

White Mountains, California

The awe-inspiring size of the Giant Sequoias led most to believe that they were the oldest trees in the world – under the assumption that the biggest must be the oldest. That changed in 1958 when Edmund Shulman, a professor of dendrochronology (the study of tree-rings), from Brooklyn, released findings of his research studying a species of pine tree growing high in the mountain ranges of California, Nevada and Utah.

The Great Basin Bristlecone Pine (*Pinus longaeva*) was long held to be ancient, and was mentioned as so by John Muir recollecting his travels in the late nineteenth century. But by counting the annual tree rings bored from Bristlecone Pines, Shulman discovered seventeen trees that had lived for more than four thousand years. This remarkable discovery changed the perspective of tree age relating to size. It became apparent that the harsh conditions found in their mountain habitat in part contributed to their longevity. Strong winds, dry, cold winters, combined with short, hot summers, leave the trees with a very short growing season, but also help reduce pests and disease which persist at lower altitudes. Growing between 2,900 and 3,050m (9,600 and 10,000ft) above sea level, the oldest trees were found in areas experiencing the harshest conditions.

Whereas most tree species hollow through decay making accurate dating almost impossible, the Bristlecone Pine shows no signs of senescence – decay caused by old age – meaning that tree rings can remain intact to the core of the trunk, thereby providing a reliable method to calculate tree age.

Shulman's findings also helped re-calibrate radiocarbon dating by providing tree ring data from pieces of slow decaying dead Bristlecone wood found to be over 11,000 years old, which had been dead for at least half that time.

Most of the trees Shulman surveyed over several summers stand in the White Mountains of Eastern California. Shulman died later the same year that he announced his discovery, and the area was preserved as the Ancient Bristlecone Pine Forest, now free to visit, accessible in the summer months once the snow has cleared.

OPPOSITE AND BELOW: Twisted, multi-coloured, fire scarred, stag-headed, ancient Bristlecone Pines 2014

There are many variable arching forms,
alone or in groups, with innumerable
tassels drooping beneath the arches or
radiant above them, and many lowly
giants of no particular form that have
braved the storms of a thousand years..

From *The Mountains of California*
by John Muir 1894

Methuselah

Ancient Bristlecone Pine Forest

In 1957 Shulman made a major discovery. By counting tree rings he confirmed one of the White Mountain Bristlecone Pines to be the oldest known living tree in the world. Many other trees around the globe make a claim on the title, but none can be proven by ring count due to internal decay, a characteristic absent in Bristlecone Pine.

Shulman named the tree after the oldest living biblical character, supposed to have lived for 969 years – a mere youngster compared to his sylvan namesake. It stands in Methuselah Grove, 15.25m (50ft) high, and just one of its three main trunks survives, sustained only by a single strip of bark. At the time of publication, Methuselah endures at over 4,500 years old.

The tree's precise whereabouts are a closely guarded secret, and it remains unmarked to protect against vandalism and prospective souvenir hunters.

In 1964, a geologist by the name of Donald Currey found an even older tree in Nevada's Wheeler Park. A 6.4m (21ft) girthed Bristlecone known locally as Prometheus caught his eye, but whilst drilling for a core section, his increment borer broke off in the tree's dense wood. After calling for assistance, a Forest Service Crew arrived and promptly felled the tree in order to retrieve his instrument.

A ring count followed and the tree was found to be 4,900 years old. Currey and the Forest Service were pilloried by peers and public alike for having destroyed the oldest known living tree in the world.

A tree ring section cored by Shulman, but left uncounted at the time of his death, was later confirmed to be from a tree 4,806 years old, and this stands as the oldest known living tree in the world, its whereabouts a secret. There may still be some undiscovered 5,000 year old trees in the Bristlecone Pine Forest, but in the scheme of things, that discovery would seem inconsequential. A walk through the Bristlecone forest is a walk through ancient history, a living history, the collective more important than the individual.

As with many other species, the Bristlecones are under threat. Fossilised remnants have been found at lower altitudes, indicating a time when Bristlecone generations moved with the climate. At present Bristlecones grow high in the mountains, and as global warming accelerates, they may find they have nowhere left to go.

ABOVE LEFT: Methuselah from the Nuremberg Chronicle by Hartmann Schedel 1493

OPPOSITE: Bristlecone Pines in the Methuselah Grove, Ancient Bristlecone Pine Forest 2014

And all the days of Methuselah were nine hundred sixty and nine years: and he died.

From *Genesis* 5:21-27

Foxtail Pines

Sierra Nevada, California

On account of its conical trunk, short branches, and short dense masses of needles Foxtail Pine shows obvious relation in its architectural form to the extreme temperature conditions and high winds of its habitat... From *Trees of California* by W L Jepson 1923

Often overlooked in favour of its more famous cousin the Bristlecone Pine, California plays host to yet another strand in its eclectic tapestry of ancient trees – the Foxtail Pine *(Pinus balfouriana)*.

Discovered before the Bristlecone during explorations by professor John Jeffrey in 1852, the Foxtail Pine shares similar characteristics; *'bottle brush tassels'* as described by John Muir, and twisted, gnarled, semi-bark less trunks as displayed by ancient specimens. It differs in that its bole becomes fat over time with thick, fire resistant bark.

Suited to a sub-alpine climate between 2,000-3,500m (6,500-11,500ft) above sea level, Foxtail forests grow at only two locations in the county; on the Klamath Mountains in northern California and on the southern Sierra Nevada – 'bear country' as the mountain signposts are quick to display.

While not quite so long-lived as its famous cousin, individual trees can reach a great age, with the oldest tree found in the southern Sierra Nevada to be 2,110 years old with a large girth of 8m (26.25ft). The large tree pictured opposite at Inyo National Forest near Mount Whitney (the highest summit in the contiguous United States at 4,421m (14,505ft), proved to be 6.6m in girth (21.6ft), placing it firmly in the upper echelons of Foxtail seniority. Specialists agree that the species could feasibly live for 3,000 years or more.

Archaeologists discovered fossilised remains suggesting vast forests of Foxtail Pine once covered a wide area across the western mountains of America some 46 million years ago, confirming the species as a truly prehistoric tree.

ABOVE & BELOW: Foxtail Pines at Inyo National Forest 2014

OPPOSITE: 6.6m girthed Foxtail Pine at Inyo National Forest 2014

The 1,000 Mile Tree
Weber Canyon, Utah

In January 1869, during construction of the Transcontinental Railroad from the Mississippi River to the Pacific Ocean, prospectors from Union Pacific found a Pine tree growing exactly 1,000 miles (1,600km) from the railroad's origin in Omaha, Nebraska.

The tree stood 27.5m (90ft) tall beside the Weber River in Weber Canyon, nine miles east of the town of Ogden. To mark the railworkers' achievement of laying 1,000 miles of track, they named it the 1,000 Mile Tree and hung a sign on it. Plans for construction of the railway had been approved by President Lincoln in 1864. It proved a monumental and hugely laborious undertaking, which while freeing the movement of people from the mid-west to the Pacific coast, displaced native Americans from their ancestral homelands and forced them onto reservations.

The pine became a tourist attraction along with Devils' Slide – a natural geographic vertical chute formed 170 to 180 million years ago – and the canyon itself. Trains often stopped at the points of interest so that passengers could enjoy the spectacle, and excursion trains were run from Ogden specifically for the purpose. Some photographs and drawings made over a century ago for postcards, books and stereocards survive the landmark.

In 1900 the 1,000 Mile Tree died, and by 1926 the canyon lost some its natural charm when it was widened to incorporate a second railway line, the Lincoln Highway and more recently the interstate road. A new tree was planted by Union Pacific in 1982 and still stands as a memorial to its forebear, and has grown to a height of 9m (30ft). The trains no longer stop here, but the more adventurous can take a canoe up the Weber River.

ABOVE: The Thousand Mile Tree 1880
BELOW: The replacement Thousand Mile Tree 2011

The Liberty Tree
Boston, Massachusets

In 1775, the American War of Independence took centre stage in world events, involving not only North America against Britain, but also France, the Netherlands and Portugal. Interestingly, the war's beginnings can be traced back to events that took place ten years earlier around a large Elm tree (*Ulmus americana)* planted in 1646 that stood by Boston Common, and came to be known as the Liberty Tree.

In 1665 the British government introduced a stamp tax on American colonists, who viewed it as an infringement on their rights. On the morning of the 14th of August that year, patriots calling themselves the Sons of Liberty met beneath the tree and hung an effigy of a British 'Redback' in its branches, along with a British jackboot displaying a sign reading 'stamp tax'. Throughout the day, crowds swelled, and speeches calling for home rule were made, in what was the first American public display of defiance against the Crown. A march followed, culminating in a mock funeral pyre where the effigies were burned. The tax collector resigned beside the tree, fearing for his life.

On September the 11th, a copper plate bearing the inscription *The Tree of Liberty* was hung on the Elm's trunk, and regular meetings took place there. The tree came to symbolize liberty in Boston.

British troops reacted by ridiculing the Elm, and paraded a patriot, tarred and feathered, in front of it. As events escalated, the tree was cut down by British soldiers, an action which effectively kick-started the revolution. The rest as they say is history.

The Liberty Tree inspired the planting of other liberty trees not only in America, but in Germany, Holland and Italy, and notably France – symbolizing the French Revolution. It surely warrants more than the brass plaque that hangs in its memory on the corner of Washington and Essex Streets.

Unmindful of names or distinctions they came,
For freemen like brothers agree;
With one spirit endued, they one friendship pursued,
And their temple was Liberty Tree.
From *Liberty Tree* by Thomas Paine 1775

ABOVE: The Liberty Tree 1886

Armed with axes, the British soldiers made a furious attack upon it. After a long spell of laughing and grinning, sweating, swearing, and foaming with malice diabolical, they cut down a tree because it bore the name of Liberty.
From *The Essex Gazette* 31st August 1775

The Treaty Tree   Philadelphia, Pennsylvania

In 1682, William Penn arrived in America from England to accept lands granted to him by Charles II, keen to establish a Quaker settlement free from persecution. He named the area Sylvania, after the Oak, Beech, Birch and Elm woodland it encompassed. It was subsequently renamed Pennsylvania by the king in honour of Penn's father, who had served as an admiral in the English navy.

Penn was a pacifist, and quickly sought to make peaceful relations with the native Lenape tribe who inhabited the area. Tradition holds that he met with elders and tribal leaders in the year of his arrival on the banks of the Delaware River at Shackamaxon, the Lenape capital, beneath a large Elm tree *(Ulmus americana)*.

There a peace treaty was made between Penn and Tamanend, chief of the Lenape Turtle Clan, sealed with an exchange of Wampun belts. No written record survives, but oral tradition and peaceful relations that endured for almost a century are testament to the agreement.

The Elm, which became a symbol of peace, prospered until March 1810 when it fell during a storm. The trunk measured 7.3m (24ft) in circumference, thought to be some 280 years old. Furniture, trinkets and ornaments made from its timber were collected avidly as relics.

In 1827 an obelisk remembering the treaty was erected in Penn Treaty Park, and in 2010, a young Elm descended from the famous tree was planted there, celebrated with Lenape singing and dancing.

Tho' time has devoted our tree to decay,
The sage lessons it witness'd
survive to our day.
May our trustworthy
statesmen when called to the helm,
Ne'er forget the wise treaty
held under our Elm.

The Treaty Tree by Richard Peters c1825

ABOVE: The Treaty Tree 1883
LEFT: The Treaty Tree by T Kelly 1843

The King sits in the middle of a half
moon, and has his council, the old and
wise on each hand.
Great promises passed between us of
kindness and good neighborhood, and
that the English and Indians must live
in love as long as the sun gave light.

William Penn 1683

We will be brethren, my people and
your people, as the children of one
father.
...between our children and our
children's children, while the creeks
and rivers run, and while the sun,
moon, and stars endure.

Governor Gordon 1728

The Senator Longwood, Florida

Don't expect to build up the weak by pulling down the strong.
Calvin Coolidge 1872-1933.

I was planning a trip to Florida to visit the largest and oldest Pond Cypress (*Taxodium ascendens*) in the county, when I heard that on 16th January 2011 the tree had caught fire and burned to the ground.

Known as a landmark by the native Seminole tribe who have lived in the area for 12,000 years, it was originally known as the Big Tree, but was re-named the Senator in 1927 after Senator Moses Overstreet donated the tree and surrounding land to Seminole County. Two years later former president Calvin Coolidge made an official visit and dedicated a commemorative bronze plaque, which was stolen in 1945 and never recovered.

The tree has been a major tourist attraction ever since, predating the lure of the neighbouring theme parks. Early visitors had to jump from log to log through the swamp to see the tree, before the building of wooden walkways that remain in place today.

Dated by core sampling in 1946, and estimated to be 3,500 years old, the Senator stood 38m (125ft) tall, with a trunk measuring 14.3m (47ft) in girth. Before 1925 the tree stood 12m (40ft) taller, but lost its top in the fury of a hurricane.

Seminole county fire fighters originally suspected arson as the cause of the Senator's demise, but further investigation suggested the tree had been struck by lightning some days before, the hollow trunk concealing the fire while it burned from the inside out. After a tip off, their original suspicions were confirmed, and police arrested local girl Sara Barnes, who had ventured inside the hollow trunk at night and lit a fire to facilitate her drug habit. She left without extinguishing the fire. By the time flames were spotted leaping from the top of the trunk, little could be done, and the Senator collapsed while fire fighters were trying to save it. Barnes received a suspended sentence, 250 hours manual labour and was ordered to pay costs totalling around $14,000.

Today visitors have to settle for Lady Liberty, another Bald cypress and close neighbour of the erstwhile Senator, which stands at 27m (89ft) tall, and 10m (33ft) in circumference, herself thought to be an impressive 2,000 years old.

In 2013 a 50ft tall tree grown from a cutting of The Senator taken in 2000 was planted at Big Tree Park so the tree can live on.

ABOVE: One of the last known photographs of the Senator taken 36 hours before its collapse in 2011

Arbol de Noche Triste Mexico City

After arriving in Hispaniola (Dominican Republic) in 1504 and serving as Mayor of Baracoa in Cuba, Spanish Conquistador Hernán Cortés travelled to Mexico in 1518 with a view to taking the lands for Spain.

In 1519, he reached Tenochtitlan, the Aztec capital of the region, where he was taken in by the Aztec king Moctezuma II, who wished to discover a weakness in his adversaries. The tables were turned when the Spanish took Moctezuma hostage, despite in essence themselves being captive within the island city. As relations soured following Moctezuma's death, the Spanish decided to escape with as much gold as they could carry under cover of darkness.

On a rainy, moonless night on the 30th June 1520, Cortés and his entourage made their way across the western causeway from Tenochtitlan across Lake Texcoco. The alarm was raised, and midway across the causeway the Spanish were met by Aztec warriors and they suffered heavy casualties. Cortés pushed on and reached dry land with a handful of horsemen. Legend tells how Cortés stopped beneath a Montezuma Cypress *(Taxodium mucronatum)*, and wept at his loss and the severe carnage inflicted on his men. With nowhere to go in a hostile land, the event came to be known as La Noche Triste (Night of Sorrows), after which the tree is named.

The Arbol de Noche Triste survived for many centuries until it was twice burnt by fire in 1972 and 1981. The giant hollow, burnt out trunk remains as a monument, centrepiece of a public square restored in 2013.

Sacred to Mexico's native people, Montezuma Cypress (known as Ahuehuete to the Aztecs), can grow to huge proportions. It represents authority, and was often planted in processional avenues. In 1910 during the celebrations of Mexico's centenary of independence, it was voted the country's national tree.

Unfortunately for the Aztecs, their victory on the Night of Sorrows was short-lived, as by August 1521 Cortés had regrouped and mercilessly crushed them.

Cortés stopped, and even sat down, not to relax, but to mourn for the dead, and think how fortune had taken many of his friends, and treasure, and he not only mourned the present misfortune, but feared what was to come, being all wounded, not knowing where to go, and without some guard and friendship in Tlaxcala; and cried not seeing death and havoc of those who triumphed.

From *Historia general de las Indias (General History of the Indies)* by Francisco López de Gómara 1552

ABOVE LEFT: Arbol de Noche Triste 1886
BELOW: Arbol de Noche Triste 1904

Arbol del Tule   El Tule, Oaxaca

Impressive as the Arbol de Noche Triste may be even in its prostate condition, the great tree almost pales into insignificance when compared with a Montezuma Cypress at Santa Maria el Tule, some 500km (310 miles) south east of Mexico City.

In 1803 Alexander Humboldt described the Arbol del Tule (Tree of Tule), also known as El Giganti, as more corpulent than the Dragon Tree of the Canary Isles or the Baobabs of Africa, and he was right. At 36m (119ft) in circumference, the tree holds the accolade for being not only the largest girthed tree of its kind, but as the largest girthed tree in the world.

Estimates of its age range from 1,000-3,000 years old, but studies conducted by the Italian botanist Casiano Conzatti in 1921 claimed the tree was between 1433 and 1,600 years old. After taking averages from other local Montezuma Cypresses, Conzatti suggested that as a rule of thumb the tree's diameter in centimetres is equal to about half its age. Interestingly, this estimate correlates with Zapotec legend which holds the tree was planted by the Aztec storm god's servant Pechoca for the villagers of El Tule some 1,400 years ago.

Trees feature prominently in the folklore of the indigenous Zapotecs, who lived in the area around Oaxaca for at least 2,500 years. In one creation myth, their ancestors are said to have risen from the earth, turned into people from two trees. In a Noah-like flood myth, Nata and his wife Nena are told by Titlacahuan, the Aztec god of destiny, to escape in a ship made from a hollowed Cypress tree.

Due to its fluted, undulating bole it was thought for many years that the tree was not one but three trees that had fused together. But in 1996, DNA testing confirmed that the Arbol del Tule was but one organism, and despite suffering from a lack of water in the late 1980s, shows no signs of relinquishing its title as El Giganti just yet.

Make no more pulque, but straightaway hollow out a large cypress, and enter it when in the month Tozoztli the water shall approach the sky.

Mexican flood myth from *The Myths of Mexico and Peru* by Lewis Spence 1913

ABOVE: Arbol del Tule c1905
BELOW: Arbol del Tule 1935
OVERLEAF: Arbol del Tule 2010

THE BIGGEST TREE.

The Columbus Tree   Santo Domingo

After five months at sea, Christopher Columbus landed his ship the Santa Maria at San Salvador on 12th October 1492. Columbus had set sail from Spain hoping to find a short cut across the Atlantic Ocean to Asia, but instead found himself in a new world, and lauded as the 'discoverer of America', even thought at the time the explorer remained convinced that he had found Asia.

The fact that the Taíno people were already well established in the Caribbean recalls to mind Ron Moody who said; *'The thing about discovery is that it was there all along'*. In fact, the notion that Columbus was the first European to discover the Americas beckons dispute – a Viking settlement was founded in the north of the continent some five centuries earlier.

By December, Columbus reached the Island known to the native Taíno tribe as Kiskeya. Much to their dismay, he renamed it Hispaniola after his homeland.

After returning to Spain, Columbus launched a second expedition the following year, with the intention of establishing permanent colonies under Spanish rule. On his return to Hispaniola, legend has Columbus sailing up the River Ozama and mooring the Santa Maria to a large Kapok tree *(Ceiba pentandra)*, on the western bank of the river. It was here in 1496 that Christopher's brother Bartholomew founded Santo Domingo, the oldest city in the Americas, following the discovery of gold.

The Taínos suffered from the new migration however. Their population was decimated both by introduced disease against which they had no immunity, and genocide at the hands of the Spanish. A Dominican superstition holds that it is unlucky to mention Christopher Columbus by name. Instead, they often refer to him simply as the Admiral.

The Columbus Tree survived as a venerated shrine until the early twentieth century, by which time it had reached huge proportions. It was pruned heavily in the 1920s due to decay, and a piece of its timber – known as balm wood by the Tainos – was presented to Mariners Bank in 1928. A new tree was planted, and has grown into a large, healthy specimen beside the stump of its slowly decaying parent.

They traded with us and gave us everything they had, with good will. They took great delight in pleasing us. They are very gentle and without knowledge of what is evil; nor do they murder or steal. Your highness may believe that in all the world there can be no better people. They love their neighbors as themselves, and they have the sweetest talk in the world, and are gentle and always laughing.

Columbus describing the native Taíno in his journal 1492

OPPOSITE: The Columbus Tree 1909

ABOVE: The Columbus Tree c2010

BELOW: The buttressed, thorny trunk of the Kapok tree. Sacred to the Mayans – the Tree of Life   they believed that it held up the sky. It has been harvested for millennia for the cotton-like fibre found in its seed pods

Bukit Timah Nature Reserve

Singapore was secured as a strategic British trading post for the British East India Company by Sir Stamford Raffles in 1819. He found it to be a sparsely populated island covered in dense jungle and swampland. Once the British secured the rights to the island from the ruling Malay sultans in 1824, Raffles set about clearing the land, commencing a project of sustained development that would continue apace to the present day.

In 1883, Bukit Timah, 12km (7.5 miles) north west of Singapore city, was one of the first areas to be established as a forest reserve. By the late 1930s, most of Singapore's forest cover had been depleted by development and logging, but Bukit Timah was retained for the protection of flora and fauna. Today, this small area of 163ha (403ac), harbours the island's largest remnant of native virgin rainforest, hosting 360 different tree species, more than the entire continent of North America.

The literal translation is bukit (hill), timah (tin), but there is no tin here at Singapore's highest point (164m - 538ft), and it has been suggested that westerners misheard 'timah' for 'timak' – a native tree that grows on the hill. A 360 year old seraya tree (Shorea curtisii) stands as the reserve's oldest.

As with most tropical rainforests, the soil here is thin, and the trees buttressed. Shallow roots retain moisture and absorb nutrients directly from the decaying leaf matter on the forest floor. Lying on the equator, the temperature is constant year round, varying between 26-28°c (79-82°f), creating a humid atmosphere.

The tigers which once roamed the hillside – reportedly responsible for almost 200 deaths in 1860 – are now gone, the last being shot in 1930. The reserve is still rich with wildlife, including 29 species of snake found only in Singapore's reserves, flying lemur, monitor lizard, mouse deer and giant ants.

A cryptid that inhabits Malay folklore is the Bukit Timah Monkey Man – a hairy grey hominid standing between one to two metres (3 to 6ft) tall, with a human gait and monkey face. It is said to be immortal and to venture out at night, so young Singaporeans were advised to avoid the area after dark. Recorded sightings have occurred since 1805, including those by Japanese soldiers during their occupation of Singapore during World War II, with the last sighting reported as recently as 2007.

Could it be that the monkey man was mistaken for one of the many long-tailed macaque monkeys that inhabit the area? I saw one prize his way through the window of a neighbouring bungalow at the forest edge, with the air of a professional cat-burglar about him.

The vegetation was most luxuriant, comprising enormous forest trees, as well as a variety of ferns...
Alfred Russel Wallace 1869

ABOVE: Singapore jungle clearance c1920
BELOW: Monitor lizard 2011
BOTTOM: Macaque monkey 2011
OPPOSITE: Bukit Timah Nature Reserve 2011

The Tembusu
Botanic Gardens

The Botanic Gardens at Singapore were established by Sir Stamford Raffles – founder of the modern port city of Singapore itself – in 1822 on the then Government Hill. His initial aim was to produce crops for profit such as cocoa, nutmeg and rubber. Moved to their present site in 1859, today the gardens are a tropical oasis of calm in a bustling city, home to hundreds of trees, including an area of rain forest and the stunning National Orchid Garden which houses 3,000 varieties of orchid.

There are fourteen heritage trees worthy of note in the gardens, but there is one tree in particular that stands out. Native to Singapore, the 30m tall (98.4ft) Tembusu tree (*Fagraea fragrans*), is as old as the gardens themselves. The girth of the trunk is difficult to measure as it undulates with large butressed roots, but the official measurement is 5.3m (17.3ft). A low branch that travels perpendicular to the tree – apparently in search of something – is characteristic of the species.

When in bloom, the cream coloured flowers open at sunset and exude a distinctive sweet aroma – hence the name *fragrans*. Its bitter red berries provide food for birds and fruit bats, and the hardwood timber is used locally to make chopping boards.

There is another, considerably larger Tembusu in the gardens that stands at a height of 42m (137.8ft) with a girth of 7.8m (25.5ft). However, with its elegant shape and the distinction of appearing on the back of Singapore's five dollar bill, this particular Tembusu has become a recognisable and iconic symbol of the island.

OPPOSITE: The Great Tembusu tree 2011

TOP: The Botanic Gardens c1920

MIDDLE: Singapore $5 dollar bill

BOTTOM: Tembusu leaves and fissured branch

216

Patriarca de Floresta

Vassununga State Park, Santa Rita de Passa

The focus of the world's attention on the plight of the Amazon Rainforest is without doubt fully merited, but it has been argued that Brazil's lesser known sister forest may be suffering in silence as a result.

Recent studies have shown that the Atlantic Forest or Mata Atlântica – which grows as a thick belt along the south-eastern coast of Brazil, roughly centred on Rio de Janiero – is now a mere shadow of its former self. Once it covered an area of 1,250,000km^2 (776,714 miles^2), but logging and development have taken their toll, and now less than 10% of the original forest remains. The urban spread of major cities such as Sao Paulo and Rio de Janiero looks set to continue deforestation, with the expected loss of up to 90 endemic animal species and 8,000 endemic plant species. The challenge is to balance ecology and business.

One such species under threat in the Atlantic Forest is the Pink Jequitibá (*Cariniana legalis*), Brazil's largest forest tree, which occupies the upper stratum of primary forest and has recently been added to IUCN (International Union for Conservation of Nature) Red List of Threatened Species.

Known coloquially as Patriarca de Floresta, (father or giant of the forest), the largest jequitibá stands in Vassununga State Park and towers above its neighbours at 49m (161ft) tall, with a girth of 16m (52.5ft). Estimated to be over 3,000 years old, it is the oldest of its kind, and possibly the oldest tree in Brazil. Ironically it was the great size of the tree that ensured its survival. When the land was cleared to be planted with sugar cane, no equipment large enough to fell the Father of the Forest was available, and so it was left for posterity. Thankfully the tree is now protected within the boundaries of Vassununga State park, where the best examples of jequitibá survive. Prime stands of the tree can also be found in the hills near Petropolis.

To a person fond of Natural history such a day as this brings with it pleasure more acute than he ever may again experience.

Charles Darwin on first walking in the Atlantic forest 1832

OPPOSITE TOP: Patriarca de Floresta 2013

RIGHT: Scene in a Brazilian forest 1855. I like to think that the Jaguar got away...

Note the similarity between the central tree and Patriarca de Floresta.

OPPOSITE BELOW: Atlantic forest near Petropolis 1999

*We spent a night at a baobab,
which was hollow, and would
hold twenty men inside.
It had been used as a lodging-
house by the Babisa.*

From *Missionary Travels and
Researches in South Africa* David
Livingstone 1857

The Big Tree Victoria Falls

The African Baobab *(Adansonia digitata)*, known as the Big Tree, at Victoria Falls is neither the largest nor oldest Baobab on the African continent (that accolade goes to the Sunland Baobab in South Africa). I include it here because it was the first Baobab I ever saw, and at a young age it left a lasting impression – looking to me like the elephantine equivalent in the plant world. My parents had visited Zimbabwe (then Rhodesia) and returned with some exciting stories and photographs, including the one illustrated here of the Big Tree.

It may not break any records, but with a girth of 16m (52.5ft), and standing to a height of 20m (65.6ft) it is an impressive sight. Thought to be 1,000 years old, it was certainly standing tall when the Scottish missionary explorer David Livingstone was shown the mighty falls of Mosi-oa-Tunya – the smoke that thunders – on 16th November 1855, which he re-named after his Queen – Victoria Falls. A bronze statue of Livingstone stands close to the Big Tree.

Livingstone greatly admired the Baobab; he measured many to try to ascertain their age. He spent a night in the hollow trunk of one on the banks of Lake Malawi, which has been named after him. Still visible are the initials DL which he carved inside the cavernous trunk. The tree is still used by locals to shelter from wild animals that roam the plains, but it is being slowly enveloped by two Strangler Figs, which left unchecked will eventually engulf their host.

Livingstone's wife, Mary, died in Africa of malaria on 27th April 1862 whilst travelling with him, and was buried under the shade of a Baobab tree. When Livingstone died of malaria and dysentery on 1st May 1873, his heart was buried beneath a Mubanga tree and his body hung out to dry on its branches, before the long return journey to London where he was buried on 18th April 1874 at Westminster Abbey.

It is known as the life-giving tree, as most parts of the Baobab have a traditional use in Africa: the bark for textile and rope, the seeds to roast and eat, the seed pods to carry water, the pith to make a refreshing drink, the leaves to cook and eat. The soft timber is made into plates. Local tradition warns that should you pick a flower from the tree, you are sure to be eaten by a lion before the year is out.

There, towering over all, stands the great burly baobab, each of whose enormous arms would form the trunk of a large tree...

From *Missionary Travels and Researches in South Africa* David Livingstone 1857

OPPOSITE: The Big Tree 1935
ABOVE: The Big Tree 1977
BELOW: Stanley meets Livingstone; 'Doctor Livingstone I presume?'

Baines' Baobabs
Nxai Pan National Park, Tutume

In 1858 the English artist Thomas Baines joined legendary explorer David Livingstone on his expedition along the Zambesi River, and with him became one of the first Europeans to see the Victoria Falls.

He had previously spent two years on a northern Australian expedition as official artist, where he painted his first Baobab trees. In 1861 he travelled to south-west Africa with the hunter/explorer James Chapman on another expedition to the Falls. The pair kept separate journals describing the voyage, including detailed descriptions of the many adversities they faced along the way. Sickness and death plagued the journey, with food and water often scarce commodities.

Setting off from Namibia on horse and by foot, Baines reached the salt pans of Botswana on Wednesday 21st May 1862, and found there an oasis of seven Baobab trees *(Adansonia digitata)*. He sat down to paint them, effectively painting himself into African history. The trees were named after him, and have since been painted by many others, including Prince Charles in 1984.

Continuing their journey, three weeks later the explorers came upon a huge Baobab engraved with the name of Canadian explorer Charles Green, who had visited four years earlier, and another Baobab, greater still at 25m (82ft) in circumference at its base. It was photographed by and named after Chapman.

Known to the natives as 'upside-down trees' (according to one African creation story, the god Thora threw one to the ground crown-first in disgust), estimates of giant Baobab's longevity vary wildly from 500 to 6,000 years. They grow quickly, invariably become hollowed with age (a tactic that enables them to store water in times of drought), and leave no discernible annual rings to count. The fact that in over 150 years the appearance of Baines' Baobabs has changed little goes some way to affirming their surmised age of 1,000 years.

A long circuit brought me, with empty pouch, to the clump of baobabs we had seen yesterday from the wagon ; five full-sized trees and two or three younger ones were standing, so that when in leaf their foliage must form one magnificent shade. One gigantic trunk had fallen and lay prostrate, but still losing none of its viatality, sent forth branches and young leaves like the rest.

From *Explorations in South-west Africa* by Thomas Baines 1864

ABOVE: 21.3m girthed Baobab Tree by Thomas Baines in Botswana 1861

OPPOSITE AND BELOW: Baines' Baobabs 2010

The Sunland Baobab

Modjadjiskloof, Limpopo

An African Baobab (*Adansonia digitata*) at Modjadjiskloof, variously known as the Sunland Baobab, Big Baobab, Pub Tree and Duiwelskloof Giant, is the largest girthed Baobab on the planet, and stands a full 33.4m (109.5ft) in circumference around its dual-stemmed hollow trunk. It is the second widest tree in the world after the Arbol del Tule in Mexico. Until 2009 another Limpopo Baobab at Glencoe held the record at 46.6m (152.8ft), but the tree split in two that year.

Estimates of the Sunland Baobab's longevity range from anything up to 6,000 years, but carbon dating of its oldest wood in 2011 provided an age of 1,060 years for the smaller stem and 750 for the larger, give or take 75 years. When you take into consideration the fact that the tree's chasm is large enough to sit 15 people comfortably, its oldest wood long decayed, it could feasibly be much older. The testing also revealed that the hollows had suffered from at least five fires between 1660 and 1990.

In the 1980s, new owners decided to turn one hollow into a pub, the other into a wine cellar, and set about clearing them out. In the process they evicted a pair of resident Black Mambas, discovered evidence of an indigenous Bushmen camp, and found some artefacts from the 1800s left by Dutch travellers who may have used the tree for shelter.

The Baobab has long held religious significance in Africa, and ancient specimens were believed to hold the Great Spirit. Young boys washed in water soaked in the bark of a Baobab were said to grow up big and strong, like the tree. The Baobab is a symbol of strength, wisdom, health and longevity.

Often described as elephantine in appearance, Baobabs share a one-sided relationship with the world's largest animal, which eats their bark, tears off their branches and sometimes pushes them over. Elephants and other mega beasts once roamed the earth widely, from Africa to northern Europe and beyond, and it is precisely this kind of rough and tumble relationship that led big trees to become so large and tough and grow thick skins, leaving the giants we see today.

(We) stopped midway to admire the first moana tree (Baobab) we had ever seen. We were lost in amazement, truly, at the stupendous grandeur of this mighty monarch of the forest.

From *Chapman's Travels in the Interior of South Africa* by James Chapman 1868

ABOVE: Baobab as spiritual totem 1914
OPPOSITE AND BELOW: The Sunland Baobab 2014

The Avenue of Baobabs Morandova

Of the nine species of Baobab known to exist, six are endemic to Madagascar, and along with 90% of its wildlife, are found naturally nowhere else on earth. The island broke from the Indian sub-continent around 88 million years ago, leaving it free to develop its unique ecosystem in relative isolation.

Known as Renala to locals (mother of the forest), the best known of Madagascar's Baobabs stand in a 260m (853ft) long natural avenue of Grandidier's Baobab (*Adansonia grandidieri*), first noted by the French naturalist and explorer Alfred Grandidier (1836-1921), after whom the species was named.

20-25 trees grow close to the south-western city of Morandova, standing up to 9m (29.5ft) in circumference and 30m (98.4ft) tall. Believed to be 800 years old, the trees were not planted as an avenue, but are remnants of the once great forests of Baobabs that today survive only in isolated groves. Added to the IUCN 2006 endangered list, their limited appearance is due to a legacy of Madagascan forest clearance for agriculture, which has occurred since the island's first habitation at least 2,000 years ago. Similar slash-and-burn practices continue today, with little or no protection for the trees future. It is thought that the island has lost over 90% of its original forest cover. Around 40% perished between 1950 and 2000. Removal of the trees threatens other members of the wildlife community including Madagascar's famous lemurs and the hawk moths that pollinate the Baobab flowers, moving in the canopy from tree to tree. They were once joined by the enormous flightless Elephant Bird, who is thought to have eaten and dispersed the Baobab seeds, but they became extinct in the 17th century.

The grandeur of the Avenue of Baobabs is something to be celebrated, a photographer's dream in the setting sun. In 2007 moves were made by the Ministry of Environment, Water and Forests to grant temporary protected status to the trees, a move which will hopefully lead to their preservation.

The body is sometimes left at the funeral home, sometimes exposed outdoors under a special hangar, sometimes hung in the forest from a tree in a basket or a mat.

Alfred Grandidier on rites of the Madagascans from *Histoire, Physique Naturelle et Politique de Madagascar* 1885

ABOVE: Madagascan Baobab at Tulear c1905
OPPOSITE: The Avenue of Baobabs Morandova 2014
OVERLEAF: The Avenue of Baobabs Morandova 2012

The Prison Tree

Derby, Western Australia

Australia has its own species of Baobab, commonly known as the Boab (*Adansonia gregorii*), but also referred to as the Bottle tree, Upside Down tree (as in Africa), Dead Rat tree, Gouty Stem tree or Monkey Bread tree (after its podular fruits).

Named after the English-born Australian explorer Augustus Charles Gregory (1819-1905), the tree is found in the Kimberley region of north-western Australia, and is easily distinguishable from its African cousins by its bulbous bottle-like trunk.

As with the African Baobab, the Bottle tree is thought to have arrived from Madagascar by sea. A seed pod is believed to have floated east some 8,200km (5,000 miles) across the Indian Ocean and landed somewhere near Derby, close to where we find Australia's most famous Boab specimen, the Prison Tree.

Sacred to the Aboriginal people and called variously Larrkarti, Junguri, Wajaar and Jumulu, the tree was a source of food, water, shade, refuge and held spiritual significance. The Boab nuts are carved and painted with traditional Aboriginal art. Recent studies suggest that the Boab's spread across the Kimberley was due to the movement of Aboriginal people, who travelled carrying its fruits as a portable food source, dispersing seeds wherever they went.

According to folklore the Prison Tree came by its name in the 1890s when a group of Aboriginal prisoners, arrested for stealing cattle, where chained beneath its shade for a night whilst en-route to the court house at Derby. The hollow tree held the bones and spirits of their ancestors.

Measuring 14m (45.9ft) around its squat, swollen bole, the Prison Tree – thought to be up to 1,500 years old – is carved with graffiti, some of it spanning a century or more, a practice the authorities have sought to deter with the erection of a rough wooden fence.

ABOVE: Australian Boab from *Illustrated Encyclopaedia of Aboriginal Australia* by William Blandowski 1857
BELOW: The Prison Tree 1960
OPPOSITE: The Prison Tree 2007

The branches of this species surround the 'gouty' stem in a circle at the top, like the heads of a hydra, and by this means form a concavity between them, which is capable of storing a considerable volume of cool, clear, rainwater. To reach this water, the natives construct ladders by simply driving a series of pointed pegs into the soft bark of the tree one above the other.

Herbert Basedow (1881-1933) Australian anthropologist and explorer, on the Boab.

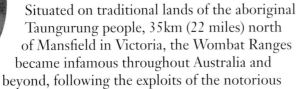

The Ned Kelly Tree
Stringybark Creek, Victoria

Situated on traditional lands of the aboriginal Taungurung people, 35km (22 miles) north of Mansfield in Victoria, the Wombat Ranges became infamous throughout Australia and beyond, following the exploits of the notorious Kelly Gang in the late nineteenth century.

The gang's leader, Ned Kelly (1854-1880), an Australian of Irish descent, was no stranger to encounters with the law. He was arrested aged only fifteen for assault, then again for aiding his mentor Harry Power with robbery, eventually serving six months hard labour for assault and indecent behaviour, followed by a further three years hard labour for receiving a stolen horse.

Following his release, the Kelly household near Glenrowan was visited by Constable Alexander Fitzpatrick in April 1878 intending to arrest Ned's brother Dan on a charge of theft. Following an altercation, Fitzpatrick left the house without his man, nursing a wounded wrist and dented pride. He reported a case of attempted murder on himself by the Kellys, for which Ned's mother Ellen was imprisoned along with two neighbours. A heavy sense of injustice led Ned and brother Dan to seek refuge prospecting for gold and rustling cattle at Bullock Creek in the heavily wooded rough country of the Wombat Ranges. It was here that a troop of policemen from Mansfield – Sergeant Kennedy and Constables Scanlon, Lonigan and McIntyre – sought to find the Kelly brothers and bring them to justice. Camped near the ruins of huts on the banks of Stringybark Creek, unbeknown to them less than a mile from the Kelly hideout, Lonigan and McIntyre were ambushed by the Kelly brothers and friends on 25th October 1878 and told to *"Bail Up"* by Ned. Unarmed, McIntyre surrendered but Lonigan drew his gun and was immediately shot dead by Ned. Kennedy and Scanlon appeared, and a gun fight ensued in which they too were killed. McIntyre managed to escape, and made his way to Mansfield to report the events.

The police murders led to the outlawing of the Kelly Gang, making them Australia's most wanted criminals.

TOP LEFT: Ned Kelly on the eve of his hanging.
ABOVE: The Kelly Tree 2012

On the west bank of Stringybark Creek, about 250m (820ft) from the official site of the shootings, stands a large Eucalyptus Manna Gum *(E.Virinalis)* with a girth of 8m (26ft), and known as the Kelly Tree.

Previously two other trees in the vicinity held the title. The first was marked by a stray bullet near to the spot where Scanlan was killed, but that large tree was felled by the Sawmill Company in 1908 to fulfil a special order for timber. In the 1930s a second Kelly Tree was posted with a sign displaying the title by the then owner of the land Charlie Beasley, but the tree died and fell shortly afterwards. The current tree was named about 1933 by a neighbour Tim Brond, who removed a section of bark and carved the names of the three murdered police troopers into the trunk in memoriam. In 1973 a small replica of Ned Kelly's armour that he wore as protection at his last stand was attached to the tree, and is close to being totally absorbed by re-growth of the bark.

In 2001, a plaque mounted on a large stone was erected as a permanent memorial to Kennedy, Scanlon and Lonigan. The site is visited by thousands of people each year.

The story of the Kelly Gang however did not end there. On 27th June 1880, after almost two years on the run and with two bank robberies under their belts, the bushrangers took hostages at the Glenrowan Inn, and intended to derail a special police forces train sent to apprehend them. The authorities were warned of the impending disaster and the trap was avoided.

Police surrounded the inn, and a furious gun fight ensued with loss of life on both sides, including some of the hostages. Ned Kelly faced the onslaught head-on during his famous last stand, dressed along with his gang in home-made armour constructed from iron plough heads donated by farmers sympathetic to the Kelly cause, of whom there were many. By shooting at his legs, the police were able to disable Ned, and he was overpowered and arrested behind a large fallen tree where he fell. The rest of the gang all died in the fracas.

At 10.00 am on 11th November 1880, Ned Kelly was hanged at Old Melbourne Goal, and buried in a mass grave.

Ned Kelly's legacy survives in some part with the Kelly Tree, but new evidence suggests that he may have had some involvement with the drivers for change for a new political system that ultimately led to the Federation of Australia in 1901, resulting in the country's independence from England.

ABOVE: Ned Kelly's last stand at Glenrowan, sporting his 'bulletproof' iron armour

BELOW: The replica Kelly armour embedded within the Kelly Tree's trunk 2012

233

The Corroboree Tree Melbourne

The trunk of a large Red River Gum tree *(Eucalyptus camaldulensis)*, stands fenced off amongst the grasses at Burnley Oval, Richmond, around 7.7km (5 miles) east of central Melbourne along the Yarra river. Long dead and hollowing – a photograph from 1933 shows the tree to be in much the same state as it is now (right) – the remains preserved as a monument to the aboriginal Wurundjeri people who have lived in the area for close to 40,000 years. The tree marked former clan territories, and was significant as a Corroboree Tree – a meeting place where aboriginals would paint their bodies and dance and sing, enacting scenes from their sacred Dreamtime – the era of the aboriginal creation stories. Outsiders were strictly forbidden at these ceremonies, but early European settlers were witness to some at this very spot. The word corroboree is itself a European corruption of the original aboriginal word caribberie, and has been appropriated.

Found throughout most of mainland Australia as one of the continent's most common trees, the Red River Gum is a fast growing hardwood that can live for hundreds of years. The Aboriginal people worked sheets of bark from the trees to make shields and canoes and build shelters. Some old trees around the city bear scars that are testament to these traditions. The medicinal properties of the tree were also harboured by crushing and boiling the leaves to produce a liniment for aches and pains and the relief of flu-like symptoms.

The remedy would do little to stave off the small pox and genocide brought to the Wurundjeri by early European settlers, against which they had no immunity.

I followed the Yarra trail along the river by bicycle from Melbourne to search for the landmark and found it un-signposted amongst stands of Red River Gums. The tree possessed an air of distinction which convinced me that I had found my subject. On reflection, what use is a sign to the Wurundjeri people? They need just call on the Dreamtime to find their way there.

He roared, stamped and danced corroboree.
From *The Water-Babies* by Charles Kingsley 1863

ABOVE: A Corroborree, Victoria c1850
OPPOSITE: The Corroborree Tree 2011
BELOW: The Corroborree Tree 1933

The Leaping Tree
Cape Reigna, North Island

When the first Polynesian travellers arrived by canoe at New Zealand's Northland around 1,000 years ago, they found a heavily forested temperate island, devoid of mammals (apart from bats), but rich in bird life.

Maori legend names Kupe as the navigator who discovered the islands, forced to flee his ancestral home of Hawaiki, fearing reprisals after leaving his cousin to drown. On landing at Taipa, Kupe's wife Hine Te Aparangi named the land Aotearoa or 'Land of the Long White Cloud', after the cloud formation that greeted them. New Zealand came to mark the southern extent of Polynesian colonisation.

For their spiritual homeland, the Maori's looked north, and on the north-western tip of New Zealand at Cape Reigna, clinging to a rocky windswept crag, is an 800 year old Pohutukawa tree *(Metrosideros excelsa)*, known as The Leaping Tree, which holds special significance for the Maori people.

On death, Maori spirits travel north on Te Ara Wairua, 'the Spirit's pathway', passing through Spirit's Bay, and on to Cape Reigna, where they descend through the roots of the Leaping Tree into the sea and on to the Manawatawi (the Great King Island), where they bid a final farewell, before returning underwater to their ancestral home-land of Hawaiiki-A-Nui.

Cape Reigna receives some 150,000 visitors a year, but access to the tree itself is forbidden. Regeneration of the headland is on-going – I planted a Manuka tree there in memory of my mother.

The European settlers dubbed the Pohutukawa as New Zealand's Christmas tree due to its bright red flowers that bloom in December – said to be the blood of Tawhaki, a young Maori warrior who fell whilst climbing for heaven. But according to legend, the sacred tree at Cape Riegna has never blossomed.

Now on the barren spirit track
Lingering sadly, gazing back,
Slowly moves a ghastly train,
Shades of warriors, brave in vain.

From *The Spirit Land* translated from the Maori poem by Judge Maning (1811–1883)

ABOVE: The Leaping Tree, Cape Reigna 2011
BELOW: Pohutakawa flowers, Great Barrier Island 2014
OPPOSITE: Cape Reigna Where the Tasman Sea meets the Pacific Ocean - Leaping Tree visible on the headland 2011

The Moreton Bay Fig
Russell, Bay of Islands

Russell, known to Maori as Kororareka, was declared a *"most noble anchorage"* by Captain Cook after his visit in 1769.

British and American whalers in need of supplies and repairs came in numbers, followed by flax traders and the deforestation of the surrounding Kauri forests – industries the local Maori exploited by trading food and women to the influx of settlers. By the early 1800s, Russell was known as the hell-hole of the Pacific, famed for grog shops and brothels – a rough, rowdy, lawless and sometime violent place.

Appalled by this den of inequity, Samuel Marsden, a member of the Church Missionary Society, met with chiefs from the Ngapuhi iwi tribe in 1814 with the intention of bringing Christianity to the native 'heathens'. It was eleven years before the missionaries made their first convert.

The Treaty of Waitangi, New Zealand's founding document, was signed across the bay at Pahia on 6th February 1840, between the British Crown and 540 Maori chiefs, drawn up for them to acknowledge Britain's governance and right for the Queen to buy Maori land, and for nine months Russell became the first capital of New Zealand.

Trade was such that a customs house was built (from Kauri) on the waterfront in 1870. Edward Binney Laing was the first collector of customs there. He reportedly jumped ship whilst mid-shipman for the Royal Navy, and planted a Moreton Bay Fig tree (*Ficus macrophylla*) at the front of the property where he worked for sixteen years. By 1900 the building was converted into a police station, the function it still performs today. I stayed next door at The Duke of Marlborough hotel which claims to hold the longest running liquor licence in the country. It formerly served as a brothel, but now reflects the town's transformation into a tranquil, peaceful retreat.

The Moreton Bay Fig tree has grown to a substantial 9.35m (30.6ft) in girth, and still produces a fine crop of fruit. Native to south east Australia, the Strangler Fig or Banyan can only reproduce with the help of the fig wasp, and may have found its way to Russell aboard Laing's navy ship.

238

A vile hole, full of impudent, half-drunken people.

Felton Mathew, a Surveyor, describing Russell c1830

ABOVE: Samuel Marsden meets the Maori at the Bay of Islands 1814, engraved 1850

OPPOSITE: The Moreton Bay Fig tree at Russell 2011

BELOW: Russell Police Station - Moreton Bay fig tree to the right of the property c1970

Waipoua Forest
North Island

Ancient of days in green old age they stand,
Though lost the beauty that became Man's prey,
When from their flanks he stripped the woods away.
From *The Passing of the Forest – A Lament for the Children of Tané* by William Pember Reeves c1890

There was a time when the great Kauri forests of New Zealand grew unhindered throughout the Northlands, stretching from the northern peninsula as far south as Auckland and beyond. The arrival of the European settlers brought such extensive logging that as early as 1900 the species was under serious threat.

The giant or king Kauri *(Agathis australis)* is a large evergreen tree that grows to 50m (164ft) tall, and can exceed 16m (52.5ft) in circumference. Found only in northern New Zealand, it dominates the forest canopy, with many other species of tree and plant living in its shade. Young trees are conical, losing their lower branches as they mature. Mature crowns host a variety of epyphites, creepers and plants, but the Kauri has the ability to shed its bark, keeping the smooth trunk free of parasites. It can live for 2,000 years or more.

Of the original forest estimated to have covered 1,200,000ha (almost 3 million ac), today less than 2% survives. It was suggested as early as 1906 that Waipoua forest in the north-west of the North Island should become a forest park – its remoteness in part saving it from destruction until then – and in 1952 it was finally declared a forest sanctuary. Here, the largest Kauri in the land survive, notably Tane Mahuta, Te Matua Ngahare and the Mcgregor Kauri – the later named after W R McGregor who successfully campaigned to end logging at Waipoua.

The 9,105ha (22,500ac) park is a popular tourist attraction and wildlife habitat, run by the Native Forest Restoration Trust and Te Roroa – the Maori guardians of Waipoua.

Tragically, the Kauri has become subject to a new threat in the form of Kauri dieback disease, which causes yellowing of the leaves, death of branches, bleeding of the Kauri gum, and eventually the death of the tree. The disease is spread by soil movement, and work is on-going to find a solution.

ABOVE: Kauri Forest 1884
OPPOSITE: Waipoua Forest canopy 2011

There was Night at the first —
the Great Darkness. Then Papa,
the Earth, ever genial, general Mother,
and our Father, fair Rangi — the Sky —
in commixture unbounded confusedly clave
to each other;
And between them close cramped lay their
children gigantic...

Alfred Domett *Ranolf and Amohia* 1872

ABOVE: Kauri leaves and cone from Kohler's
Atlas c1850

LEFT: Tane Mahuta, Waipoua Forest c1930

OPPOSITE: Tane Mahuta, Waipoua Forest 2011

Tane Mahuta
Waipoua Forest, North Island

Named after the Maori atua (god) of the forest, Tane Mahuta – Lord of the Forest – is the largest, best known and most visited tree in New Zealand.

Standing 45.2m (148ft) tall, with girth of 15.44m (50.6ft), and a trunk that barely tapers – typical of the Kauri tree – Tane Mahuta is thought to be between 1,500 and 2,000 years old, and could predate the arrival of the first Polynesian travellers to the island by 1,000 years. No wonder then that the Kauri giants held such a powerful place in the native psyche, symbolizing both greatness and strength.

According to Maori mythology, in the beginning Rangi the Sky Father lay in the arms of Papa the Earth Mother, in the expanse of darkness that was Te Poo, the night. Their children, the gods, lived between them. Craving freedom and light, the Gods efforts to separate the pair were unsuccessful until one son – Tane – prized them apart using all his strength with his hands on his mother and his feet on his father. The ensuing light and space inspired Tane to bring his own children – the trees – into the world to clothe his mother. But Tane planted the trees upside down. Realising his mistake, he tore up a giant Kauri tree, and shaking the soil from its branches, replanted it roots down. For his next trick, Tane filled the great, green canopy of the forest with birds, and lived among them with his brothers.

Feeling remorse for having separated his parents, Tane placed the sun on his father's back to warm him, and the moon before him. He also clothed Rangi in a garment of glowing red, but deeming it unworthy, removed it. Part of the garment remained though, and can still be seen at dusk as the glowing sunset.

In the 81 years between my photograph and the archive picture illustrated, the great Tane Mahuta has barely changed, affirming the longevity of the tree.

243

ABOVE Giant Kauri with a girth of 13.7m (45ft)
Waipoua Forest 1908

OPPOSITE: Te Matua Ngahere, Waipoua Forest 2011

244

Te Matua Ngahere
Waipoua Forest, North Island

Less than a mile from Tane Mahuta stands Te Matua Ngahere – Father of the Forest – another remnant from the forest of giants, a survivor of the European lust for Kauri timber.

At 37.4m (122.7ft) tall, the tree is somewhat shorter than Tane Mahuta, but the circumference of the trunk measures 16.76m (55ft), giving it a superior girth – the largest of any tree in New Zealand – and therefore more annual tree rings, which when counted after extraction by auger in the 1950s, aged the tree at over 2,000 years – the oldest living Kauri tree.

The Father of the Forest was discovered in 1928 by Nicholas Yakas, who was working on the development of Highway 12 – the only main route through Waipoua Forest.

A boardwalked track leads to the tree, constructed to relieve pressure on the surrounding plant life from the thousands of annual visitors, and particularly to protect the delicate root system of the Kauri.

Maori tradition recalls the tale of the whale and the Kauri: The whale admired the giant of the forest from the sea, and in turn, the Kauri admired the giant of the sea from the forest. Through mutual respect the pair became friends. When fearful that the tree would be felled for a canoe, the whale asked the Kauri to join him in the ocean. He declined, explaining that he would drown in the water. The whale too was tied to his world, unable to survive on dry land. They decided to exchange skins, which is why the bark of the Kauri is thin and grey – as full of resin as the whale's is of oil.

As with Tane Mahuta, up to fifty plant species thrive in the crown of the tree, including orchids and ferns and until July 2007, a Strangler Fig – but that parasite was blown to the ground in a storm, along with Te Matua Ngahere's leading branch, leaving a large gap in the canopy. The event could shorten the life of the Kauri by centuries, but does nothing to dent the awesome presence of the tree, so for me, the Father of the Forest is most definitely 'the daddy'.

Kauri logging, conservation and regeneration

Archaeological evidence suggests that early Maori forest clearance took place some 900 years ago. However, it was not until the arrival of the Europeans in the eighteenth and nineteenth centuries that huge swathes of Kauri forest would be lost.

The first recorded Kauri felling occurred in 1772 at the Bay of Islands when Marion du Fresne, a French explorer, took a tree for his ship's foremast. Before he could leave, he met his death along with 26 members of his crew at the hands of Maori warriors, who killed and ate them for breaking 'tapu' by fishing in forbidden waters at Manawaroa Bay. Retribution resulted in further blood-letting on both sides that continued for another three years.

Captain James Cook explored the coast in 1769 and noted fine stands of timber that would make good masts for his Royal Navy warships. When looking for Kauri, the timber inspector to the navy Thomas Laslett noted; *"The largest I ever met with was one standing near to Mercury Bay, which measured 80 feet to the branches and 72 feet in circumference."*

ABOVE: Kauri logging 1888
BELOW LEFT: Kauri logging at Wairoa Falls, Wairoa River 1905
OPPOSITE: Kauri canopy, Waipoua Forest 2011

Kauri was easy to work, and its durability made it ideal for ship and house-building. First the smaller coastal trees were felled. Then, as the industry expanded, timber merchants moved inland where the giants stood. Trees were felled in the most inaccessible places, the huge logs dragged by oxen or driven down river via Kauri dams.

By 1897, 75% of the Northland Kauri forests was devastated, and today only 2% survives. It was not until 1973 that depletion and public opinion forced a government ban on Kauri felling, and in 1987 the Department of Conservation was created, and is effectively protecting the tree. Until recently, it was an offence to fell Kauri without special permission, but relaxation of planning regulations has seen several high profile cases where mature Kauris were almost lost. Some timber comes from the buried trunks of ancient fallen Kauri trees that have lain submerged for some 30-40,000 years. Thought to have been felled by cataclysmic earthquakes and volcanic activity, the trees have been preserved in their dormant state thanks to a ph value of 7 in the earth. When dug up, although no longer retaining its tensile strength, the ancient Kauri can be worked as new timber, and is used to make furniture, ornaments and even musical instruments.

Its remarkable properties, twinned with the rarity of the timber ensures that the Kauri available demands an equally remarkable price.

Kauri gum

A by-product of the Kauri trade was Kauri gum, the hardened fossil resin from the tree. The Maoris used it to light flax torches, and the Europeans found it to be useful in the production of varnish and linoleum. It was collected in huge quantities and became New Zealand's principal export.

At first the lumps of gum could be picked up freely from the ground. When these supplies ran out, further stocks were found just below the surface, then a foot deep, and finally up to fifteen feet down and requiring substantial excavation, illustrating the existence of many former ancient Kauri forests.

Huge swathes of the Northland countryside were turned over for Kauri gum extraction, but the industry went into decline in the 1930s when synthetic alternatives were found to be more cost-effective.

Kauri gum was also extracted from living trees, bleeding naturally from wounds and accumulating in the crown. But 'gum bleeders' soon found that they could harvest gum by cutting notches into the trunk. The practice inevitably caused the death of the tree, and was banned in 1905.

Today, Kauri gum is used for making ornaments and jewellery, as it can be polished to a high finish, and is considered to be New Zealand's alternative to amber, which it resembles in appearance.

OPPOSITE: Kauri gum bleeds from a living tree, Puketi forest 2011

BELOW: Kauri regeneration on Great Barrier Island 2011, where the Kauri Timber Company resolved to fell 'every tree over 12 inches in diameter'

In the sighted, blighted North
where the kauris grow,
And the earth is bare and barren
where the bush-bee used to hum,
And the luck we've followed's failing
And our friends are out of hailing,
And it's getting narrow sailing
by the rocks of Kingdom Come,
There's a way of fighting woe,
squaring store-bills as you go,
In the trade of digging gum.

From *Song of the Gumfield* by William
Satchell 1896

Easter Island
South Pacific

Easter Island, or Rapa Nui as it is known by its native population, marks the eastern extent of Polynesian colonisation. It is also the most remote of the Pacific islands, lying some 3,700km (2,300 miles) west of the Chilean mainland.

Oral history has Rapa Nui's first chief Hotu Matua arriving in his double hulled canoe sometime around the year 1,200. He was met by a richly forested island, harbouring over twenty species of tree. Predominant were around 16 million endemic Easter Island Palms (*Paschalococos disperta*), the largest Palm tree in the world, growing up to 30m tall (100ft), and 3m (9.8ft) in girth. The settlers set about clearing the forest to farm their staple sweet potato and yam, and used the palm logs for fire wood and sea-faring canoe masts for fishing, palm fronds to thatch their stone houses, and bark that was fashioned into clothing. Logs were also used

in part to move the hundreds of Moai – the great megaliths for which Easter Island is famous – and bark was turned to ropes to pull them into place on their coastal platforms known as Ahu. As the design of the Moai developed, it is thought that later models were literally 'walked' along, held upright with ropes.

Between 1250 and 1650 deforestation for agriculture continued apace, helped in no small part by rats introduced to Rapa Nui by the Polynesians. By eating the Palm nuts, young shoots and tender roots of the trees, the rats helped kill many more whilst inhibiting re-growth.

When the first European visitor, Dutch Navigator Jacob Roggeveen approached on Easter Sunday 1722 – hence the Island's name – only a few small groves of trees were visible. At the time of Captain Cook's arrival in 1774, barely a tree remained. By then the Islanders no longer had the materials available to build canoes and were effectively marooned in the South Pacific, patching up their last remaining ageing craft with driftwood.

All the natives frequently and actively repeated the word 'miro', and grew impatient when it was not understood at all: this is the name of the wood used by the Polynesians to make their canoes. ...vessels that sail the Pacific Ocean will have no interest in going there since they will find no water or wood;
Abel Dupetit-Thouars 1840

LEFT: Engraving of the Rano Raraku quarries on Easter Island from L'Univers Pittoresque c1850 after an original by William Hedges, the artist on Captain James Cook's expedition of 1774

By 1880 following European settlement, the Easter Island Palm had been felled to extinction, lost along with its once-thriving population of sea and land birds. The fragile soil eroded without the forest root systems to hold it in place.

Another endemic tree found on the island was the Toromiro *(Sophora toromiro)*, and like the Easter Island Palm was thought to be extinct. When Thor Heyerdahl visited on an archaeological expedition in 1956, he was directed to the sole survivor of the species in the sheltered crater of Ranu Kao, an extinct volcano in the south west corner of the island. It was in poor condition, so he took a cutting back to Sweden for analysis, where in 1959 seeds were germinated at the Botanical Garden of Göteborg. Since that time efforts have been made – so far with very limited success – to re-introduce the Toromiro to Easter Island.

Known locally as Miro, the small, yellow flowered leguminous tree once flourished on the island and was held sacred by the islanders. They used it to carve wooden figures known as moko, inscribed

tablets with petroglyphs called rongorongo, and as planking for building canoes.

The introduction of a large sheep population by European settlers sounded the death knell for Easter Island's last remaining first growth trees and ensured re-growth was entirely halted by the effects of over grazing. The islands indigenous population was also devastated – forced into slavery and susceptible to diseases introduced from Europe, against which they had no natural immunity.

The story of Easter Island is an often quoted example of localised ecological disaster – natural resources depleted beyond repair by over-harvesting through un-sustainable methods. Whichever way you look at it, Easter Island is a poignant reminder of our fragile world and a lesson in global conservation to preserve and protect the precious little that remains.

ABOVE RIGHT: Moai at Rano Raraku
ABOVE: Toromiro on Oahu 2010

Bibliography & further reading

Amazon Past, Present and Future, Thames and Hudson (1992)

Barnes, Ian, *Historical Atlas of the Celtic World*, Cartographica Press (2009)

Bassett, Sinclair, Stenson, *Story of New Zealand*, Read (1992)

Camacho, J P, *Guanches, Legend and Reality*, Weston (2012)

Collins Gem Trees, Harper Collins Publishers (1980)

Cotterell, Arthur, *Norse Mythology*, Sebastian Kelly (1998)

Davies, Norman, *Europe – A History*, Pimlico (1997)

Drinkwater, Carol, *The Olive Route*, Weidenfeld & Nicolson (2006)

Eli, Gordon, *King Kauri*, The Bush Press (1996)

Evelyn, John, *Sylva, Vol. 1 or A Discourse of Forest Trees* (1670)

Great Barrier Island, Canterbury University Press (2004)

Isaacs, Jennifer, *Australian Dreaming*, Lansdowne Press (1988)

Johnson, Hugh, *The International Book of Trees*, Mitchell Beazley Publishers Ltd (1973)

Johnson, Owen and More, David, *Collins Tree Guide*, Harper Collins Publishers (2006)

Keane, Arthur, *Japanese Garden Design*, Tuttle (2004)

Lanner, Ronald, *The Bristlecone Book*, Mountain Press (2007)

Lansley, Belinda, *The Lancashire Witch* (2013)

Larner, Jim, *The Oakwoods of Killarney* (1992)

The Last Rainforests, Mitchell Beazley Publishers Ltd (1990)

A Landscape of Myths and Narratives Madonie Cultural District (2012)

Linford, Jenny, *A Concise Guide to Trees*, Parragon Books (2007)

Lowe, John, *The Yew Trees of Britain and Ireland*, Macmillan and Co. (1897)

Mysteries of Easter Island, Thames and Hudson (1995)

Packenham, Thomas, *Meetings with Remarkable Trees, Remarkable Trees of the World, The Remarkable Baobab*, Weidenfeld & Nicolson (1996, 2002, 2004)

Pocket Trees, Dorling Kindersley Ltd (1995)

Rackham, Oliver, *Woodlands*, Collins (2006)

Rain Forests, National Parks & Wildlife Service, Sydney (1977)

Reed, A W, *Aboriginal Myths*, Reed (1988)

Reed, A W, *Maori Myth and Legend*, Read (1996)

Spence, Lewis, *The Mysteries of Britain* Senate (1994)

Strutt, Jacob George, *Sylva Britannica* (1826)

The History Box, Hermes (2001)

Trees, Dorling Kindersley (1992)

Trees, Timbers and Forests of the World, Leisure Books (1978)

Wilkes , J H, *Trees of The British Isles in History & Legend*, Frederick Muller Ltd (1972)

Woodward, Marcus, *The New Book of Trees*, A M Philpot (c1920)

World Atlas of Archaeology, Mitchell Beazley (1988)

Popout Maps & Guides www.popoutproducts.co.uk

Berlitz, DK Eyewitness, Marco Polo, Rough Guides

About the author

Julian Hight trained as a graphic designer and musician. His interest in trees started at a young age as he was lucky enough to grow up close to woodland which had a profound effect on him. He has spent most of his working life in publishing and is currently a freelance author and graphic designer with a passion for ancient trees. World Tree Story is his second book, following Britain's Tree Story for National Trust in 2011.

Julian campaigns to save threatened trees and ancient woodland, and is an active member of the Woodland Trust and Ancient Tree Inventory. He currently lives in Somerset. For further information visit:

www.worldtreestory.co.uk

Useful websites

In the course of my research, I trawled a myriad of websites, too numerous to mention The following proved invaluable:

www.monumentaltrees.com

www.ancient-tree-hunt.org.uk

www.ancienttreeforum.co.uk

www.woodlandtrust.org.uk

www.ancient-yew.org

www.treehunter.co.uk

www.venerabletrees.org

www.nonington.org.uk

www.ancientforestalliance.org

Picture credits

All photographs, postcards and engravings are from the private collection of © Julian Hight, or in the public domain, except for the following, for which I gratefully acknowledge permission to use in this book:

p28: © The Fawcus Family
p34 top: © www.panteek.com
p42 bottom: Rory Francis
pg 54 top: © www.skane.naturskyddsforeningen.se
pg 92 bottom, pg 123: David Hight
pg 93: top right © www.kimberleythomas.com
pg 93 top: Charlotte Woodall
pg 105 bottom: Jake Hight
pg 106: Francesco
pg 114 top: © www.petrohrad-obec.cz
pg 125 right: © Agricultural University of Athens
pg 126 bottom: © Katerina Karapataki
pg 147, 149: © Konstantin Hoshana
pg 155: © The Sisters Olive Trees of Noah, Bechealeh, Lebanon
pg 174 bottom: © T J Watt www.tjwatt.com
pg 204 bottom: Shane Karstens
pg 212: © Library of Congress
pg 213 top: © Janette Keys www.colonialzone-dr.com
pg 222 top: Copyright © RBGKew
pg 222 bottom: © Karen Capindale
pg 224 bottom & 225: © Peter Aldred
pg 227: © Janet McCrae
pg 232 right, 233 bottom: © Bill Denheld www.ironicon.com.au
pg 236 bottom: © Hazel Benson
pg 238 bottom: © Karen Jahn
pg 251 right: © Aurbina

The following © State Library of Victoria www.cedric.slv.vic.gov.au:
pg 192 right, pg 232 left, pg 233 top, pg 234, pg 240, pg 246

The following © www.shutterstock.com: pg 81: © msgrafixx, pg 151: © Zvonimir Atletic, pg 159: © erandamx, pg 160: © Lec Yiu Tung, pg 175 bottom: © Andrea Izzotti, pg 210: © Vadim Petrakov, pg 223: © Hannes Thirion, pg 228-229: © Dudarev Mikhail, pg 231: © mumbojumbo

The following Creative Commons CC Attribution-ShareAlike images from www.commons.wikimedia.org:
pg 70: © Rellingen, pg 145 top: © Rice University, Houston
pg 153: © www.oregonstate.edu, pg 157: © Biswarup Ganguly
pg 158 bottom: © Sophie Voillot, pg 172: © Chris 73, pg 207: © Jonclift, pg 218 top: © Bruna Leone Gagetti, pg 230 bottom: © Philiphist, pg 251 left: © David Eickhof

Above and beyond

For invaluable support: Charlotte Woodall, Jake Hight, Harry Hight, David Hight, Vince Parker, John Evans, Louise Woodall, Stephanie Bramwell-Lawes, Anna Carr, Sylvia May.

For inspiration, research and travel assistance:
UK - Jill Butler, Germany - Barbara Marnau, Crete - Katerina Karapataki, Sicily - Jane Hawkins and Alfio, USA - the Phillips family, Don Bertolette, David Burg, Tom Kimmerer, Annalee Allen, Japan - Kyoko Iwasa, NZ - the Benson & Blackwell families, AUS - Greg Bedford, Derek & Julia Parker, Bill Denheld, and all the fabulous people I met on my travels.

Roll of honour

The following pledged via an Indiegogo crowdfunding campaign, whose support enabled production of this book:

Georgie Allen
Colin Ashley
Peter Berridge
Janice Brown
Cate Browne
Jonathan Buck
Lucy Burkin
Kathi Churchill
Andy Clark
Jason Clark
Lola Clark-Stone
Rebecca Cole
Steve Cole
Gary Collinson
Nick Cooke
Blaze Cyan
Adam Davies
Bill Denheld
John Dutton
Ian Edwards
Rosita Elias
Gareth Evans
Pat Evans
Lois Fearman
Pat Feeney
Sonia Follows
Jennifer Furnell
Steve Gant

Pippa Goldfinger
Anthony Hammond
Vincent Hastings
Grania Hayes
Margaret & Michael Hendries
David Hight
Louise Hight
Anna Hillman
Spencer Holliday
Elizabeth Hope
Chris Humphrey
Alison James
Tom Joye
Tim Kellett
Elizabeth King
Alexandra Klevenz
Ruth Knagg
Leslie Zehr
Emma Maguire & Dave Turner
Mary Mannion
Nicola Mascall
Janet McCrae
Marc Meyer
Crysse Morrison
David Moss
Jane Murray

Zainab Nigoumi
Ott
Jay Pittman
Joe Port
Anthony Rogers
Danny Rose
Kerry Silva
Amani Skillen
Richard Swann
Gareth Thomas
Ieuan J Tranter
Malgorzata Tyczynska
Sue Walpole
Nick Waterhouse
Ann & Peter White
John & Sue Williams
Alan & Nancy Wilson
Chris Woodall
John Payne Woodall
Louise Woodall
Mark Woodall
Becky & Eddie Young

Index

Tree Species 🍃